The *New* China

MONEY, SEX, AND POWER

PHILIPPE MASSONNET

translated from the French
by Hannah Taïeb

TUTTLE PUBLISHING BOSTON • RUTLAND, VERMONT • TOKYO

First published in English in 2000 by Tuttle Publishing, an imprint of Periplus Editions (HK) Ltd, with editorial offices at 153 Milk Street, Boston, Massachusetts 02109.

This edition is published by arrangement with les Editions Philippe Picquier, Arles, through le Bureau des Copyrights Français, Tokyo.

Library of Congress Cataloging-in-Publication Data

Massonnet, Philippe.
    [Chine en folie. English]
    The new China: money, sex, and power / Philippe Massonnet; translated from the French by Hannah Taïeb. — 1st ed.
       p.   cm.
    Includes bibliographical references.
    ISBN 0–8048–2116–X
    1. Social change—China. 2. China—Social conditions—1976–I. Title.
    HN733.5.M36613   1999   99–41591
    306'.0951—dc21   CIP

Distributed by

USA
Tuttle Publishing
Distribution Center
Airport Industrial Park
364 Innovation Drive
North Clarendon, VT 05759-9436
Tel: (802) 773-8930
Tel: (800) 526-2778

Canada
Raincoast Books
8680 Cambie Street
Vancouver, British Columbia
V6P 6M9
Tel: (604) 323-7100
Fax: (604) 323-2600

Japan
Tuttle Publishing
RK Building, 2nd Floor
2-13-10 Shimo-Meguro, Meguro-Ku
Tokyo 153 0064
Tel: (03) 5437-0171
Fax: (03) 5437-0755

Southeast Asia
Berkeley Books Pte Ltd
5 Little Road #08-01
Singapore 536983
Tel: (65) 280-1330
Fax: (65) 280-6290

First edition

06 05 04 03 02 01 00   10 9 8 7 6 5 4 3 2 1

Design by Dutton & Sherman

Printed in United States of America

Driven by extraordinary energy, Asia is in a process of spectacular transformation: in spite of their diversity, each country is swept on by a wave of economic growth envied today by the West. There is no model system, however, and no harmony either, but a multiplicity of exchanges and distributions, and therefore conflicts, paradoxes, and also inequalities.

Behind the certainties, far from stereotypes and the easy, hasty, and over-simplifying syntheses, certain elements are even to be evaluated; the sense that this newly acquired prosperity can generate enough real gain to outweigh the risk of fracture and disenchantment.

It is the researchers, journalists, and press correspondents from large foreign editorial offices who will present to the reader, one by one, the many facets of contemporary Asia in the news reports that enable us to think about and understand the current disruptions and what is at stake. For "in the field" observers with a critical mindset—whether it is about the Chinese mafia, the Japanese bureaucracy, or the new Vietnamese society—it is the goal to give the reader the keys to decipher what is taking place, to share in the emotions and even the major questions for the future.

—

ACKNOWLEDGMENTS

Thanks to Fang Fang and Paul Tian Qiu for their patience
and support; to friends for their advice; and the Agence France-
Presse from whom I obtained precious material for the writing
of this book.

Contents

Foreword

On February 19, 1997, the news spread through the world at the speed of light: Deng Xiaoping, the father of Chinese economic reform, had died. The work of the Chinese patriarch is indeed compared and contrasted. But whatever the regard held for his intolerance with respect to the dissidents of his country, he leaves behind a China in full economic and social turmoil. This book arrives therefore at a timely point to establish a first assessment of this silent revolution. And what an assessment!

China—one quarter of humanity. The prognosticators worldwide are all focusing on China's vastness because it is clear that China has become the big question mark for the future. It is no longer a matter on which we can remain indifferent since the choices of today in this country will weigh heavy tomorrow on the rest of humanity in the economic, social, political, and strategic domains.

For a long time China provoked fascination, curiosity, and romanticism in the West. In 1295, when Marco Polo returned to Venice and published his *Book of Wonders of the World,* his contemporaries refused to believe in the reality of this powerful and brilliant China he described there. Seven hundred years later, the Westerners arrive dumbfounded by the extraordinary economic development of this continent which continues to arouse envy and fear.

Increasing envy in the business domain, rightly or wrongly, sets people dreaming about a new commercial El Dorado in a world of economic crisis. But increasing fears in political environments leads Europe and the United States to do everything so as not to bother the sleeping dragon. Is this the best choice?

Be that as it may, what astonishing revenge of the people subjected to and colonized by Westerners in the nineteenth century. A terrible shock which would precipitate the end of the imperial dynasties and later thrust the country into tragic bad habits from Maoism. Thirty years after the cultural revolution and twenty years after the death of Mao Zedong, the coastal provinces post rates of growth over 15 percent a year. The highest in the world! As for the humiliation of colonization, it is almost gone with the triumphal return of Hong Kong to Chinese sovereignty.

But if the increase in power of China is formidable, it is not necessary to make a fuss about it. Let us not hypnotize or fool ourselves. Although in full development, China remains a developing country. It has overall doubled its gross domestic product in fifteen years—a remarkable performance. Per inhabitant, the country still only ranks seventy-ninth in the world with a gross domestic product of 422 dollars. Moreover, no one will swear that China will be in a position to pursue, on a long-term basis, the current pace of its development. All the more so, this economic takeoff creates considerable social upheaval in the interior of the country.

Even the most optimistic people of the West are obliged to dilute their opinions. To say, as did the prestigious World Bank, that China will be the first economic power of the world in 2010 or 2020 is a farce. In reality, an observation is easy to make: to predict the future of China is a perilous exercise.

Far from making crazy plans, Philippe Massonnet has applied himself to describing the reality of today. It is presented here, with tenderness and irony, in a series of colorful and impertinent descriptions of a China in folly; a jungle where the law of the strongest imposes itself on the most weak or where the unrestrained rush to money upsets traditions and mentalities. Materialism triumphs over ideology. Individualism is victorious over community. An immense wave of consumerism takes everything in its path. In this China of post-Deng Xiaoping, only the immediate well-being counts.

Many books, scholarly or otherwise, have tried to analyze the immense Chinese enigma. This one is the first in a long time that shares with us directly and with emotion the daily Chinese life. The Chinese from all sides; the poor peasants who descend upon the cities in the hopes of earning a living there, the new capitalists, millionaire bosses who are in charge of horrible factories where employees are exploited, the young women who "sell their smiles" behind the screens of brothels, the spoiled only children who are granted everything they want.

But if the ideology is moribund, the regime still clings to power. Almost ten years after Tiananmen, this China that charges along at great speed without knowing too much about where it goes will present a situation of enormous concern in the West. Democracy and personal human rights, do they have the same meaning in Paris as in Beijing or Tibet? At a time where a muffled battle in Beijing takes place among the "old regime", the "new regime," and the "modern regime," between the authoritarians and the democrats, to understand more deeply what happens in this country is essential and indispensable to us.

—Pierre-Antoine Donnet

Introduction

What do a Beijing merchant, a Cantonese Communist Party official, and a Sichuan peasant have in common? The desire to get rich by any means possible. One of the rare freedoms enjoyed by Chinese people today is the freedom to make money. In the country of "market socialism," everyone knows, or thinks, that he or she can become a millionaire overnight. Wasn't it Deng Xiaoping who kept saying, "It is glorious to get rich"? The people of the Middle Kingdom don't need to be told twice. This is the only slogan they apply to the letter. Fervently, wildly, they're out to make it.

Workers, champing at the bit to fatten up their skeletal bank accounts, are deserting state companies for a booming private sector. Underpaid professors cut classes to pursue more profitable activities. Peasants leave the land for towns and cities, eager to conquer the promised land that television promotes ever more enticingly. Even the People's Liberation Army is getting in on the act: Not content just to modernize, the army produces condoms and ice cream. As for politicians, they're relishing the dizzying intoxication of taking bribes. Everyone wants to go into business—or, to use the expression in style in the 1990s, "to take the plunge" (*xiahai*)—literally, "to throw yourself into the ocean." To abandon your state job, your "iron rice bowl." Entrepreneurs of the world, unite!

China in the 1990s resembles an immense around-the-clock construction site. The economy is bubbling over. Since 1992, when Deng Xiaoping drastically accelerated economic reforms, industry and commerce have shown staggering growth. The whole world has its eyes riveted on the new economic dragon. Flush with success, this nation of 1.2 billion people sees itself as the major world power of the twenty-first century.

The Chinese have to fight to get ahead. This means changing old habits. Gone is the welfare state, fostering carelessness and laziness. Egalitarianism and social solidarity have been relegated to the museum of communism. It's every man for himself—and beware of "losing face."

Women, even more than men, have found in economic liberalism unprecedented possibilities for emancipation. For the most talented, it's paradise—and for millions of others, it's hell on earth. In China, everything can be bought and sold, even women and children. Prostitution flourishes in every season, in every region; so do AIDS and other sexually transmitted diseases. Crooks of all kinds, pimps and thieves, want their slice of Papa Deng's pie. Organized crime, maintaining unnatural relations with the Communist Party, pulls the strings— and everyday violence is a part of the new landscape.

The frantic race for money is matched by a wild consumerism. Department stores have become favorite destinations for the "popular masses." Sometimes people just go window-shopping, but often they engage in mind-boggling shopping sprees, totally out of proportion to their paychecks.

Revolutionary slogans, once omnipresent in Chinese life, have been replaced by cloying advertising slogans—just as ubiquitous, and as sticky, as overcooked rice. Bombarded by these invasive ads, the Chinese dress better, eat better, buy racing bikes, and take taxis. The well-off take their driver's test (or, better still, just buy their license) and treat themselves to cars. Ring roads are popping up everywhere. So are traffic jams and polluted skies. In the city and in the country, the environment is deteriorating.

The Chinese could care less. They're too busy consuming. They're too busy fixing up their spanking new apartments in the suburbs created from real estate speculation and corruption. Why shouldn't officials fill their pockets, since they're members of a party that is now communist in name only? High-level officials drive around in black-market Mercedes while traditional dwellings tumble before the bulldozers, to be replaced by pretentious office towers, symbols of a modern, dynamic, prosperous China. Not that people are happy about losing their old homes. Sometimes there's resistance against the most egregious of these evictions.

Still, a modern apartment's not a bad thing. The Chinese today have more living space, too, since family size is shrinking, due to population control. Rural families may try to slip in a few extra children, but city people tend to conform to the rigid family planning restrictions. In the apartment reigns the emperor, the only child, for whom the parents bleed themselves dry, whose every wish is their command—even if this little Son of Heaven stands only as high as three litchis! When the parents fall short in their duties, the grandparents are never far away. By 2050, the over-sixty crowd will make up a quarter of the population—a worrisome boom in grandparents that is a direct consequence of the birth control initiative. Who will pay for the retirement benefits of the 400 million elderly people in the middle of the coming century? No one knows.

The Chinese are living for the moment. They're spending money, they're having fun—as they never could under Mao, as was difficult even during the 1980s. Everywhere karaokes and nightclubs are replacing workers' clubs. Another sign of the rise in the standard of living: the Chinese have begun to buy pets. Cats and dogs prance around in housing projects, no longer symbols of a bourgeois lifestyle. (Still, many people prefer them piping hot on a plate!)

Not everyone is satisfied with this consumers' paradise. Many fear the futility of a society based on the freedom to make and spend money—a freedom that is bound to shrivel up when the economy slows down—and call instead for political freedom. Even if they despise the reign of money, they know that money is still indispensable if they are to finance their struggle for democracy and human rights. The dissidents have gone high-tech: rather than sticking up *dazibao* (large character posters), they're sending faxes and tapping away on the Internet, to the chagrin of the political police.

The state invests heavily in Tibet and Xinjiang, the far reaches of the empire, in order to placate "national minorities" who consider themselves to be colonized. When money is not enough to calm the ardor of the "hostile elements," there's always repression. The people's communes have been dismantled, but the gulag has not been. And despite some progress in judicial matters, the government continues to imprison and execute Chinese citizens arbitrarily. A bullet in the neck seems to be the regime's only response to the astonishing rise in crime—and it doesn't work.

In China there's a widening income gap between developed and underdeveloped regions and even between rich and poor people of the same region or city. Economic liberalization hasn't only created winners—far from it. Disparities lead to social conflicts, which threaten the fragile unity of this gigantic country, where the slightest problem becomes a question of state. The Communist Party, torn by internal discord among officials who are often more interested in money than politics, finds it harder and harder to control the explosive situation. As if seeking pardon for having massacred its youth in 1989, the Party is allowing the Chinese people to do just about whatever they want in their daily life, as long as they don't voice any criticism of the regime. This tactic is not without risks, but that's the price the Party has to pay for its intransigent refusal to make the political system more flexible and its insistence on preserving its own power.

Short of capital to fuel its economic transformation, China hasn't hesitated to call "foreign friends" to come to its rescue. Foreign businesses have been fighting to get in line at the foot of the Great Wall. At the same time, the government's propaganda departments are flooding the country with ultranationalist slogans. It's paradoxical: On the one hand, the Chinese people have long had tendencies toward xenophobia, and on the other hand, there's a fascination for the West, a movement to give up cultural traditions and imitate the "barbarians." Censorship of the media and of cultural works may limit Western "pollution" but can't eliminate it. The new China-based "spiritual civilization" that leaders call for daily seems elusive.

Hong Kong, returned to China on July 1, 1997, gave the Chinese government the long-dreamt-of opportunity to sound the trumpets of nationalism and declare its revenge on imperialism. Operation Hong Kong was carried out at full speed.

In fact, everything is moving quickly. Getting rich quick has become the only goal of a depoliticized and disoriented people whose spiritual and ideological guideposts have disappeared. Yet on the surface, they have never been happier. These are China's mad years, and the Chinese are living them to the full. They're out of breath. Living in a dream.

In the pages that follow, four citizens tell the story of today's China: Zhang Donghua, a postal clerk turned millionaire; Yao Guoguang, a frustrated professor; Xiao Bai, an ambitious concubine; and Sun Lin, an uprooted peasant woman. Their daily adventures whirl us into the eddies of a society where everything is changing at once, and we share in the national drunkenness of a people gone mad, caught up in the unbridled race for money.

The original French edition of this book was written between 1996 and 1997. For the English version, we have brought some passages up to date without attempting to incorporate all of the economic and social changes that have come to pass. In China, things change quickly; but as of this writing, in August 1998, the overall trends remain the same. The race for money is still just as frantic. China is still going mad.

Through the lives and stories of the four main characters, this book seeks to evoke the delirium of this country at the dawn of the third millennium. The author, a journalist and a traveler, speaks Chinese and spent almost ten years in China, including four as a correspondent for Agence France-Presse in Beijing. He has met these women and men, symbols of turn-of-the-century China. Without them, and other anonymous Chinese people, this book would never have been written. Thanks to them all.

Chapter *One*

MONEY IS KING

"It's not the Communist Party card that opens doors these days, Dad, it's the credit card. THE CREDIT CARD! Do you hear me?" There. He had said it. In fact, he had screamed it. Zhang Donghua had finally found the courage to announce to his parents that he was giving up his "iron rice bowl"—his job as a civil servant. Zhang easily could have gotten his Party card. Instead, today it is a credit card that he has tucked in his Western-brand black leather wallet—a little trifle that cost him what the average worker sweats to make in three months.

Zhang has become a millionaire—a winner—someone who knows how to take advantage of "socialism with Chinese characteristics." Nothing about this ex-postal worker from Beijing suggests his high destiny. He is moderately intelligent and average looking, his only distinctive characteristic being a wily, flirtatious glimmer in his right eye. He has become one of those men and women you see on every street corner of every city in China—a motor of the economy, envied by the masses and spoiled by the government. Until 1985, Zhang was the second-in-command of his section in a post office in Haidian, the university neighborhood. For ten years he worked there, ate there, and took his showers there. (He didn't have a bathroom at home.) He played cards there, even though it was theoretically forbidden, and he tried to pick up his colleagues, even though that was "not healthy," as his bosses put it. They themselves didn't hesitate to try their luck with the young female staff, whose menstrual periods were posted in the family planning office.

There was no shortage of work at the post office, but there were so many extra workers that each employee could occupy a part of his or her time in some way other than sorting letters and stamping money orders, activities that are not particularly fulfilling even for the dullest of Chinese functionaries. And Zhang was far from dull. Deep inside, he knew that he was not meant to spend his life at the post office. As a member of the "lost generation" whose studies were interrupted by the Cultural Revolution (1966-1976), he had landed in this career almost by accident. He could just as easily have become a tax official or a policeman. As an adolescent, he had dreamed of being the first Chinese person to walk on the moon. The American imperialists had done it—why not one of the Red Guards? According to Mao, they were invincible—until the day when the Great Helmsman found that the joke had gone on long enough, and he asked the army to calm down the millions of excited youth who had been naive enough to swallow his teachings whole.

Instead of a spaceship, it was a black Flying Pigeon bicycle that launched Zhang every day into his postal orbit. He cursed his stuffy office with its moldy green walls and sputtering fluorescent lights that hung from an infuriatingly low ceiling. He detested his coworkers, who were "soft as mushy melons" and competed with each other in ingratiating themselves with the bosses and dreamt of a quick rise through the ranks and entry into the Party. The Chinese just say, "Get into the Party," as if it were obvious that they could never belong to any party other than the Communist Party. In fact, there are eight other political organizations. Allies of the Communists during the civil war, they were permitted to continue to exist after the founding of the People's Republic. These parties are given honorary seats, giving the impression that they influence the life of the country. Without challenging Communist hegemony, these groups provide the appearance of a more congenial political landscape for inattentive foreigners. The Party counts 50 million members; the eight other parties 300,000....

Oh, to join the Party! A privilege, a sacred rite! If a man becomes a Party member, his parents' tears of joy are enough to make the Yangtze River overflow. His father lingers each day a bit longer in front of his building, slowly pushing his bike with a disingenuous air, praying that the neighbors are watching him and dying of envy or, better still, that they will offer a word of congratulations for the child prodigy, the hero of the family, the neighborhood, the quarter. Someday maybe he'll be a model national worker, decorated in the Great Palace of the People in Tiananmen Square, his name cited as an example in all the factories and popular communes in China, his picture hanging in all of the workers' clubs from Beijing to Canton and from Shanghai to Lhasa. A fabulous destiny, more proof that socialism is the most advanced system in the world!

Glory and, above all, "face" were not the only reasons motivating Chinese people to join the Party in the 1980s. Except for a minority of sincere political zealots, most candidates were after the material advantages. Of course, simple Party members did not enjoy the same favors as established officials; but all members could hope for better housing, access to hard-to-get products, and even a passport. Members of the Party could also hand down to their children a legacy that was supposed to protect them against political persecution. Accustomed to the excesses of their leaders, the Chinese know that the official line could reverse itself from one day to the next. It is better to possess an acceptable "class origin" to control the damage. And, if possible, a Party card.

Zhang hated himself when he thought of the future that was mapped out for him. *Petty, small-minded, gutless*—these words echoed loudly in his head as, robotlike, he stamped savage blows with his postal stamp. He was all the more worried because although he was not part of the impressive army of workers courting the officials in his work unit, he was nonetheless very well thought of by his superiors. They appreciated the conscientiousness with which he carried out whatever task he was given. Zhang dreaded his bosses' proposal that he join the Party. If he continued working hard, at thirty-five he could become head of his post office section—a remarkable achievement which, although it would not be published in the *Guinness Book of World Records,* would surely be mentioned sooner or later in one of the post office's many gazettes. In his thirties, he had two options: he could make a lifelong commitment to the system and sign on for a life that would be just barely comfortable but without any major worries, or he could jump ship while there was still time. He chose the second option, taking advantage of a favorable political and economic climate.

1985. After the first years of economic experimentation of the Deng Xiaoping era, China finally committed itself to an apparently irreversible path. With the Party headed by the liberal Hu Yaobang, the government seemed sincere in its desire to reform the economy and to allow the Chinese people free enterprise. "Get rich" was the message Deng drummed into them, being careful to specify that even if he was uncontestably number one in the country (at last), he wasn't God. There would be no miracle. No, no, no, China wouldn't swing over to capitalism, he insisted—but it was inevitable that certain people would get rich more quickly than others. It was necessary for the Chinese to get rid of their welfare mentality slowly, warned Deng. He was an admirer of America, where his children and grandchildren were to study and work. Fine, Zhang had thought. But there was no need to go to America. He'd make the transition right here in Beijing.

"The day I announced to my parents that I was leaving the post office to 'take the plunge,' I thought my mother was going to have a heart attack," Zhang remembers, laughing. "I was still living with them because I wasn't married, so I didn't have the right to a place to live. The post office had offered me a place in the dormitory, but I had refused it. It was Sunday evening at about 6 P.M., the first of July, and it was pouring rain. My mother was silently preparing wonton soup in a nook in the house that we use as a kitchen, and my father was watching the Beijing Opera on TV in the bedroom/living room. When I let it drop all of a sudden that I was quitting my job in order to sell leather clothes with a friend, my mother thought for a moment that I was kidding. It wasn't the first time I had mentioned how sick I was of being a postal clerk and my desire to stand on my own two feet. When I insisted and came out with the details of my plan, she finally realized that I wasn't kidding. And I could see catastrophe looming. In a matter of seconds, her face, normally very dark, turned white—as white as her wonton wrapper. She started to gasp for breath, and beads of sweat appeared on her forehead. I screamed. My father leaped up from his armchair and came to my mother's aid. What a scene! My parents, both civil servants, didn't understand how I could give up job security, free health care, and the free oil and fish distributed to my work unit for Chinese New Year and the national holiday. When my mother came to, my father tried to get me to change my mind, and the tension started mounting. The discussion went downhill. Since it was the anniversary of the date of the founding of the Communist Party, I threw out my phrase about the credit card and the Party Card. I got it off my chest. Nowadays, my parents are my strongest supporters."

OUTWARD SIGNS OF WEALTH

Gone are the days when one hid one's money for fear that the Red Guards would steal it in the name of class justice. These days, if you've got it, you flaunt it. The only question is how far a person will—who will do the most indecent striptease. Money has become *the* reference point and modesty the worst of sins. Zhang has made the most of his money. First there are his two cars, the most obvious of his status symbols: a Mercedes 600, which he drives himself although he has more than enough money to afford a chauffeur, and a Toyota Corona. Then there's his luxury apartment in the modern nouveau-riche neighborhood of Fangzhuang, perched high over Beijing. The locals call the area "Beijing's Manhattan" and the Chinese government likes to bring foreign guests there to demonstrate the success of the country's economic reforms.

Zhang lives in a duplex that is of 120 square meters (the average floor space per city dweller is 7 square meters in big cities). His home is luxuriously decorated and furnished: wood floors, marble, and the latest appliances and electronics, including a wide-screen TV that he virtually never watches.

The powerful and respected businessman also owns a villa on the tropical island of Hainan, south of Canton. He selected one of the new wealthy zones of the provincial capital and built a house. Regarding the architectural style, it's safe to say that it's flashy and in doubtful taste; beyond that, it's hard to pin down. It is reminiscent of Louisiana architecture in color and materials, of the Anglo-Saxon ilk with Roman columns.

At the beginning of the 1990s the special economic zone of Hainan was a tax haven and a land of conquest for real estate promoters. It was there, in 1994, that the government, looking for a new-style hero, came up with the youngest millionaire in the country, a certain Xuan Duxing. At the age of thirty-three, this ex-immigrant worker, son of a peasant, had become king of the building industry—a success story that sent the official press into paroxysms of joy.

Zhang is happy just to be one of the one to two million millionaires counted by the tax department in 1995. (There were only 500,000 three years before.) His fortune allows him to live a life that is princely compared to that of the huge majority of his fellow countrymen and the rest of the population of the planet as well.

He has a wife he doesn't love, whom he wed when the time to marry had come and gone, and a son born in 1988. He splits his leisure time between his friends and his child, who is being raised primarily by paternal grandparents and a governess. Zhang meets his friends at his private club—the kind of place that was unknown in the Middle Kingdom until recently, unless you count the fortresses of the dignitaries of the regime. The membership fee: 50,000 yuan (at the end of 1996, 100 yuan was equivalent to US 308 dollars) plus an annual payment. In the sauna or bar of the club, one talks business, of course, all kinds of business, and exchanges the latest gossip and anecdotes circulating in this extremely closed circle. Stories such as this one: rich entrepreneurs of the special economic zone of Shenzhen, in Guangdong province, had organized a contest for the most expensive meal in the fanciest restaurant in town. The prices kept rising and rising until the management of the establishment couldn't think of anything else to offer their capricious clients. One of the restaurateurs came up with a great idea and ended up being crowned champion: he had all the food covered with gold dust. This true story appeared in several local newspapers, and apparently the papers had their hands slapped for having reported, without the slightest reproach, this shameful waste.

Only women who work there are allowed into the sanctum of the club, so mistresses wait elsewhere. Zhang is a bit of an exception because he does not have an official "concubine," but he doesn't hesitate to go out of town with a call girl from time to time. His wife knows about it but doesn't say anything. This forbearance is part of their arrangement. In exchange, Zhang doesn't interfere with her private life and lets her spend money as she sees fit. She doesn't hold back.

Zhang made his fortune in the clothing industry in less than five years. Then he began to speculate, without knowing much about what he was doing. He started out like most Chinese, thinking of the stock markets of Shanghai and Shenzhen, created at the beginning of the 1990s, as if they were casinos or racetracks, and pouncing on shares as if he were betting at blackjack or backing a horse. Some Chinese pocket considerable earnings using this approach, but others are ruined. These extremely speculative markets can turn around completely from one day to the next, bankrupting those who have made fortunes.

After two or three close calls, Zhang plunged into the study of stock market techniques in order to invest as intelligently as possible given the volatility of the markets. He read specialized books sold in state bookstores and then moved on to American works translated into Chinese (he doesn't read English) that his friends brought him back from the United States.

It was around that time that he met the extraordinary Xie Yuan, who became his associate for a while. Of Zhang's generation, with the same ambition and the same taste for risk, this Shanghai native with his baby face and piercing gaze had an address book almost as thick as the six collected volumes of the selected works of Mao. Somehow Xie managed at the same time to be boss of his own prosperous business, a stockholder in various firms in all parts of the country, a representative of a famous Western firm, a procurer, and a delegate of the Communist Youth League of one of the sectors of the great eastern metropolis.

Shanghai seems to give birth to people of this ilk. It's not the only city in China to do so, but it seems to play a special role in fostering such businesspeople. The frenetic economic development of the "Paris of the Orient," as Westerners called this port city at the beginning of the century, has encouraged all the excesses in a population that wants to get back its own. The first industrial center of the country, Shanghai had to wait until the beginning of the 1990s to free itself from the state that had been milking it for forty years. The city had all of the financial and human attributes needed to build success, many of them inherited from the colonial era. Shanghai's first attempt at revenge on Beijing came in 1966 when Jiang Qing, Mao's wife, and her acolytes, the Gang of Four, made Shanghai their headquarters for the great proletarian Cultural Revolution. If at the outset the movement gave a bit of pride to the people of Shanghai, it was no more beneficial to them than to the rest of the population. The consequences were actually rather catastrophic because Beijing got back at Shanghai by digging even deeper into the till of the city after Mao's death in 1976.

The acceleration of economic reforms in 1992 and the rise to power of the "Shanghai clique," with Jiang Zemin as head of the Party and head of state, got the city back on track.

No one today denies the essential role Shanghai has played in the Chinese economy. It is the commercial and financial beacon of the country. Its standard of living is one of the highest in the country, higher than in Beijing's. The residents of Shanghai, residents of the biggest city in China, consider the Northerners to be peasants who don't understand the slightest thing about business. Inevitably, this sudden economic liberty has made some of the citizens of Shanghai giddy. With malicious pleasure they jump through the gaping holes in the lax legislation on economic and financial matters.

Xie Yuan is a perfect example. He was an able inheritor of the business talents of his father and grandfather who held prominent posts at the Shanghai and Hong Kong bank during the nationalist regime. Charming and gutsy, he made as much of a hit at urbane cocktail parties as he did at political meetings targeting corruption and decadence. Zhang met this phenomenon, a pure product, like himself, of Deng Xiaoping's reforms, not at a Party cell meeting but at a Shanghai "health care center" with very pretty nurses on call. Thus was born a collaboration not unmixed with friendship. It was more like a mutual admiration society, linking an entrepreneur and a master of deception. The pair worked together for a year—until the day Xie got arrested for procuring during an anti-vice campaign. He would have gotten away with this offense, wily as he was, if only he had not refused to "lend" one of his girls to a vindictive police commissioner. Xie was detained for only twenty-four hours, but the story got around, making it to the corridors of Zhang's Beijing club. In spite of the two or three brilliant financial deals he and Xie pulled off together, Zhang decided to break off what had become a risky connection.

At the club, one can share one's little secrets, as long as the personal information revealed can't be used against one of the other members. The Chinese business community is not a martial arts temple wreathed in higher wisdom but a boxing ring where half the blows are illegal and below the belt. When they're not talking about money, businessmen like to talk about their health, which is going downhill as their bank balances rise. The previous economic system never encouraged people to take on responsibilities and work hard; therefore those individuals who "took the plunge" are now finding the demands of business painful physically as well as psychically. Very rapidly, high blood pressure has become the number-one chronic deadly illness, and the number of diabetics quadrupled between 1979 and 1994. Overwork, lack of physical exercise, food that's far too rich (even when not sprinkled with gold dust), and the abuse of alcohol and tobacco are to blame.

China has 35 million smokers, almost all of them businessmen who see the cigarette (foreign brand, Virginia tobacco) as an integral part of who they are. The result is one death per minute from the effects of tar and nicotine, particularly deadly when combined any old way in cigarettes made in illegal factories specializing in counterfeiting well-known foreign brands. Two million deaths per year from cigarette smoking are projected by the year 2025. Experts confirm that health expenses related to tobacco use surpass the admittedly juicy state revenues brought in from the sales of the 150 billion cigarettes smoked every year. Big cities have started to create nonsmoking zones in public places, and the central government has voted in a law forbidding tobacco advertising in sports arenas. But the law is easy to get around. Perhaps such intemperance is understandable. It's as if the Chinese people, so long deprived, have suddenly found that their country is full of dusty Aladdin's lamps; when you rub them, gold issues forth.

Overwork, anxiety, disappointment, and bankruptcy have led to a surge in the number of reported cases of mental illness and suicide, touching not only businessmen but laid-off workers and indebted peasants. In China, as elsewhere in Asia, personal failure is experienced as a veritable social humiliation, much more so than in the

West. Since the end of the 1980s, the biggest cities have set up coun-seling centers and telephone help lines for people in distress. There are also radio call-in shows for those who need moral support.

Although his ulcers may give him a twinge from time to time, Zhang has no regrets. When he sees his old post office colleagues, now Party members, he can't help but despise their baseness and lack of ambition. Parking his limousine as close as possible to the entrance of his old workplace gives him enormous pleasure. How many phony smiles, groveling bows, and cartons of cigarettes did it take his col-leagues to secure their ridiculous little two-room apartments, mea-gerly decorated with cheap calendars ornamented with inaccessible pinup blondes and badly printed posters of alpine meadows or the Golden Gate Bridge! Most of them will never set foot in their dream-lands, while he—little Zhang, ex-second-in-command of his section, he with the unruly right eye—can take off tomorrow for Honolulu or Paris if he so desires. Business class, of course.

Zhang has remarked that at the post office, as elsewhere, people are not fighting so hard to obtain that famous Party card. The Chinese have other ways to achieve a better life. When Deng Xiaoping got the economy going in 1992, he made it possible for the lucky, the resourceful, and the brave to cut the umbilical cord that tied them to the welfare state. For better or for worse.

FRUSTRATED INTELLECTUALS

Like Zhang Donghua, Yao Guoguang approves of economic liberaliza-tion. The two men, however, have little else in common. Yao, a univer-sity professor nearing retirement, with the build of a football player and an overblown manner of speaking, also frequents the Haidian post office—not to snub ex-coworkers, but simply because he lives in the neighborhood. He has a little two-room apartment, which he rents for a modest sum from his employer. It's a typical Chinese home, which he shares with his wife, who is a secondary school teacher. In the bathroom, which is constantly damp because of faulty plumbing, you'll find no marble—just badly laid pink ceramic tiles covering the bottom half of an off-white wall with peeling paint. A room of two and a half square yards contains—barely—a sink hardly bigger than a soup bowl, a toilet designed to accommodate Lilliputians, a light green pipe fitted with an unmovable shower head of yellow plastic, and a washing machine by Haier, the famous Sino-German appliance company. How did the Yaos manage to fit all that in there? It's amazing the number of things the Chinese manage to squeeze into apartments the size of pocket handkerchiefs!

With only ten hours of classes to teach per week at the university math department, Professor Yao has plenty of time to dedicate to his "second career." Like most city dwellers—with the exception of private entrepreneurs and perhaps also employees in the service sector, whose official employment provides a reasonable revenue—the professor has one official job and another one under the table. Or rather, several others. Tutoring provides a considerable financial contribution, but the professor can also transform himself into a chemist, a computer consultant, or an electronic engineer. It depends on the day and on the job offers. He doesn't claim to have any real competence in these areas, but he banks on the air of authority that is conjured by the title of mathematician. He sells himself unhesitatingly to businesses looking for miracle solutions to avoid declaring bankruptcy during this period of very intense economic competition. For him, as for other civil servants, he earns more in his second career than in his official one. The average salary of an official employee or worker is 500 yuan a month—enough to survive on—but Chinese people today are looking to profit from the enticing new consumer society.

"My salary as a professor is 500 yuan. With bonuses and overtime, I can make 600 or 700. Soon I'll be sixty! What can you do with that? Even with two salaries, it's not so great. Do you know how much a wool sweater costs? At least 200 yuan. A washing machine? 2,000 yuan. A car? 100,000 yuan," the professor exclaims. With the exception of the car, which is still a luxury item, most Chinese in big cities still manage to put together a complete set of appliances.

Workers in floundering state businesses sometimes receive only part of their already meager salaries. Most public firms are operating on a deficit, and more and more are shutting up shop, temporarily or permanently. "The iron rice bowl," the symbol of job security for the last forty years, has broken, and no one will ever put the pieces back together again. Those in need—supposedly temporarily, but often indefinitely—must have a second career in order to make ends meet. Luckily, the unbridled economic growth of the 1990s has generated a stream of jobs in the private sector. For the urban poor, hit hard by the steep rise in the cost of living—years of double-digit inflation—the state is gradually putting into place special "safety net" subsidies. The big cities are establishing a similar system at the local level and employment agencies are multiplying. *Unemployment* was a word that didn't appear in the Maoist vocabulary; during de-Maoization, the word was replaced by the modest phrase "waiting for work." But today the authorities acknowledge the reality of unemployment. It is impossible to deny the evidence. The rate of urban unemployment will be higher than 7 percent in the year 2000—from a mere 3 percent in 1995. This means that there will be 20 million urban unemployed at the end of the century, according to the most optimistic official predictions.

The government hesitates to give the go-ahead for massive shut-downs of state-run agencies and factories because it is afraid of creating social turmoil and endangering the political regime. Factories and state organizations employed 140 million people at the end of 1996, so the growth of a worker protest movement would be a dangerous thing. Not quite sure how to control the potential damage, the government is encouraging companies to change their management style in order to adapt to the market, hoping thus to save the ones that are the least badly off. But any ruthless social planning meets with resistance, sometimes violent, which the official and only union rushes to sabotage to protect Party authority.

The profound restructuring of the economy has launched a chaotic race for money—a race with as many losers as winners, a race run by people of every milieu and every age. Besides food, what is the favorite subject of conversation in China? Money. Every conversation includes a figure or a sum. Even Professor Yao's students wish they were studying business or international economics rather than literature or mathematics. But in the university, as in the army, one doesn't choose one's post. As long as the liberal arts are devalued morally and financially, more and more young people will drop out in order to "take the plunge," at the risk of drowning later on. Why linger in the classroom when dropouts can become billionaires? That's what the students say to themselves. The teachers, themselves chasing madly after money in their spare time, are ill suited to convince their students that learning is the key to success in the new society.

Take professor Yao. What's his ideal? The same as that of Zhang—making money. His two children now married, he has all the time in the world to dedicate to making money to lavish on himself and on his beloved granddaughter, and satisfying her whims costs him dearly.

Unlike Zhang, Yao was not in the Red Guard. He was too old. A junior professor labeled "rightist" because of his family origins—his father and grandfather were in the Kuomintang—he spent two years rotting in prison during the Cultural Revolution. After being rehabilitated along with millions of other persecuted people who survived assassination attempts and "suicides," he won the right to become an underpaid professor. A few years earlier, during the Great Leap Forward, in 1960-1961, he learned what it was to go hungry. Like all Chinese of his generation, he grows a little crazier every day fixating on the possibility of getting rich quick. He's perfectly willing to admit it: "The Chinese are crazy, especially professors," he says, exploding with a burst of laughter that could make the Great Wall tremble.

He's less amused when he thinks of his official status. He may be pleased that the authorities no longer put dunce caps on professors to humiliate them (a well-known practice during the Cultural Revolution), but he knows that teaching is not a profession appreciated by his fellow citizens. True, professors and teachers have their own national holiday every year on September 10, when the regime rewards "model teachers," but during the rest of the year, teachers win little respect from pupils and parents. Many teachers are fed up. Why accept a job that is socially important but pays quite poorly in an environment where there is no freedom of expression and the working conditions are deplorable? "If you want to find a school in a major Chinese city, it's easy. Just look among the most run-down buildings," the professor exclaims with a touch of bitterness in his voice. While the gross domestic product of China has grown at a devilish pace these last few years, money spent on education has fallen proportionately.

For all these reasons, the teaching profession is attracting fewer and fewer young people. Professors lack motivation, so they lose their students' confidence. A study by the Institution of Pedagogical Research in Shanghai in 1994 showed that only 11 percent of youth consider themselves to have good relationships with their teachers, while two-thirds of teachers judge the students intolerable. It's a real crisis. There has been a snowballing of resignations, like that of Xiao Mei, a young woman who taught natural science in a high school in Beijing. She slammed the door on her institution (which was no worse than any other), worked selling luxury leather goods for a while, and finally found a job as an assistant in a big foreign car firm, where she earned a salary six times greater than her teacher's salary.

In the countryside, desertions by teachers have reached record levels. The salaries of professors and teachers there are about half those in the cities, that is, when the teachers are paid at all.... Like some agricultural workers, some teachers are paid with vouchers when the local coffers are empty. They are often empty. Local governments cannot entirely compensate for the financial disengagement of the central government, and in any case they often prefer to spend public funds on projects that are more commercial in nature. Overall, the number of primary schools in the country has fallen by 250,000 between 1970 and 1992. The fall in the number of births is not sufficient to explain this decline.

To make up for the lack of funds, the government exhorts schools and universities to finance themselves. Now that the state pays for no more than about 30 percent of their operating costs, the schools have to get along as best they can, by renting out their buildings to businesses, for example. "It is not rare for professors to band together and rent their own offices to private companies and then share the revenue," explains Professor Yao. Many educational institutions have created businesses, including stores and restaurants—a risky solution, since such investments don't always pay off, and school directors in the People's Republic of China do not often turn out to be good managers. Most schools and universities turn to a simpler solution: They raise the cost of tuition. They do so despite the fact that such costs traditionally have been extremely low in Communist countries, and an education law adopted in 1995 sustained the principle of free education. Nonetheless, in the country of "socialism with Chinese characteristics," some public schools charge prohibitive rates that bear no relation to the quality of education provided. These rates can reach as much as 10,000 yuan per year—which is what the average Chinese person makes in a year. The government's reaction is to fret and fume, threatening to punish the most outrageous abuses. The ineffectiveness of this response underlines the lack of authority of central power in the provinces.

This daunting situation appears to be a threat to the existing requirement of nine years of education for all Chinese. Nonetheless, the government maintains its ambitious objective of eliminating illiteracy by the beginning of the twenty-first century. Officially, the number of illiterate people has fallen from 80 percent in 1949 to 15 percent in 1990—there are 180 million illiterate people, two-thirds of them women, most of them living in rural regions. The reduction in illiteracy is a remarkable feat, if the figures can be trusted, but the current decline in public schooling will make it difficult to sustain this progress. Private schools cannot be counted on to resolve the crisis.

Thousands of private grade schools, high schools, and universities have been founded since the beginning of the 1990s. The tuition is several thousand yuan per month, at best. The rich province of Guangdong has more than six hundred private schools, thirty of which fall under the "luxury" category, with costs to families of 150,000 to 300,000 yuan for five years of study. How can one justify the existence of such institutions in a country where the principle of equal opportunity is still part of the official discourse? The principals of private schools don't waste their time on convoluted reasoning. "It's simply a matter of meeting the particular needs of one category of families," declares an official at one of the most elite schools in Beijing. Zhang's son goes there. Some of the little boarders at this school are the children of Chinese people who have temporarily gone abroad, but most are the children of businessmen and business-women who live nearby.

Why did Zhang, the ex-postal employee with the Mercedes 600, decide to send his son to a boarding school, only to see him on weekends? "It's a lot better equipped than the state schools. The classes are not overcrowded and the professors are well-paid and so they're conscientious. I don't see why I should enroll my son in a class of fifty students with a teacher who is wondering what he's doing there and spending his time cooking up schemes to make ends meet instead of preparing his courses. Besides, in private school, the kids eat well. In the public cafeterias, they give them one bowl of rice with three lousy scraps of meat smothered in a foul mash of overcooked vegetables, crowned with a steamed bun that's not even stuffed!"

Professor Yao would agree. "Frankly, our salaries are crappy," he often says, meaning his own, of course, as well as those of his col-leagues, and more generally all civil servants.

Their salaries are no longer enough to cover care in the event of an emergency. Professor Yao found that out one evening when he was hit by a car while carelessly crossing the big avenue that runs alongside the workers' stadium. He will never forget that night at the hospital— it would have made a great Marx Brothers movie.

PUBLIC HEALTH IN JEOPARDY

There was no ambulance. In spite of an obvious fracture in the lower part of his left leg, Professor Yao was thrown into a little taxi by a taxi driver and the driver of the car that had knocked him over. They chucked him in with about the same amount of care a garbage collector takes in throwing garbage into the back of his truck. The twenty or so gawkers flocking around the victim stood unmoving—arms crossed, leaning on their bicycles, retelling the event like sports announcers doing an instant replay. No one helped. At moments like this, one can see the extent of the damage wrought by one of the most collectivist and authoritarian systems in the world. It has created generations of self-centered individuals for whom solicitude is possible only when it's obligatory. As the last vestiges of socialism disappear, individualism, so long repressed, resurfaces.

Even more striking was the indifference with which the injured man was greeted on his arrival at the Jishuitan hospital, considered one of the best in the capital.

It was 8 P.M., and he was in the emergency room. No orderly on the horizon, no stretchers, either. No nurse to help the professor out of the car. The taxi driver and the driver of the car that had caused the accident went off in search of a stretcher. The receptionist in the main entrance hall, who was really more of a cashier than anything else, had the "I could care less" attitude typical of any state employee. Finally, on the second floor, the two men found an abandoned stretcher in a hallway. Judging from its worn-out condition, it could have been used during the Sino-Japanese War.

Fast-forward: The evening, still absurd, was becoming less and less amusing. The driver, having loaded his patient on a rusted and rickety cart, finally found an intern. After a blasé "expert" glance at Professor Yao, barely taking his cigarette out of his mouth, the doctor did the patient and his attendants the favor of filling out the necessary form, all the while scratching his greasy hair with a persistence that suggested that a good shampoo was badly needed. With this form, already crumpled but correctly stamped, the driver went back down to the cashier to pay a hundred yuan or so. Payment precedes any care, and the sum is the same for all, rich and poor. A half hour later, the driver was still paying, at another cashier, for the X ray of the accident victim, who, meanwhile, was lying on his stretcher in the corridor trying to forget that his leg hurt like the devil. The pitiful state of the other patients did not make it any easier for him to forget his own pain.

The X ray itself was a surreal experience. The technician, still young but already disillusioned, was clearly not inclined to venture beyond the bounds of his function of photographing human insides (a badly paid job, it is true). He had no intention of hoisting the professor onto the X-ray table. The daughter and son of Professor Yao, who had since arrived, painfully laid out the 220-pound injured man on the table. The stoicism of the imperturbable technician proved that the situation was not unusual.

Then, once again, it was time to wait along with the traffic accident victims, the hoodlums with knife wounds, the exhausted street people, and the beat-up prostitutes. At midnight, it was time for the plaster cast. Another scene from a slapstick movie: the doctor begged for help from Professor Yao's children, who plunged their hands into a huge sack of plaster while the other patients looked on in astonishment. The night had just begun. Once the patient had swallowed the tranquilizers, the doctor sent him into a big cold room, a kind of parking lot for sick people waiting for a bed. That evening, the parking lot was jam-packed. The professor's family had to make several calls before they found an institution that could take in their father—a small hospital in the diplomatic neighborhood of Sanlitun.

There, although the night nurses' welcome was not exactly warm, it was more courteous than in Jishuitan. But the family was immediately sent to the cashier to make a down payment of 3,000 yuan. Looking ahead, the children had brought with them this sum, which is equivalent to seven times the patient's monthly salary and well more than his savings. Three thousand yuan—more than the annual income of many peasants.

Before the professor was taken to this room, his daughter, not without difficulty, had to wake up the one intern. Dozens of raps on the door finally roused him from his deep sleep. At three in the morning, Professor Yao finally got to lie down on a bed. Half a bed, to be exact. In this run-down and badly heated room, another patient was already bedded down between the dirty, smelly sheets.

Were these two hospitals exceptions to the rule? Had the professor had bad luck? No. Compared to the few modern institutions reserved for the political and propaganda elite, the public health system throughout the country is pretty pitiful. This hard reality brings home the fact that China is still a developing country in many ways. It's poor. The wealth that trickles down here or there merely hides the problems.

The state budget for health, like the budget for education, has been substantially cut. The state wants hospitals to be run more rigorously, to manage their budgets according to liberal economic principles—to make up for the deficits that accumulated during the Maoist period. The government will no longer run to the aid of hospitals that are losing money. Long live "the responsibility system"! But most health-care institutions are in a catastrophic situation financially, a legacy inherited from the previous system set up by the same party that is still in power. What does the government suggest? That hospitals transform themselves into share-holding institutions, call on private capital, including foreign capital, and raise the price of health care sold to patients. Mao's barefoot doctors must be turning in their graves. Mao's successors seem to have set themselves the goal of destroying everything he had achieved. In the name—supreme hypocrisy—of the same ideology, socialism.

In 1993, the one-hundred-year anniversary of the birth of the Great Helmsman, the traitors who inherited Mao's mantle put an end to free medical care for employees in the public sector, a generous policy that was instituted by Mao in 1951. At that time only 4 million people were covered. The sixfold increase in health-care expenses between 1980 and 1993 convinced the new masters of the country to terminate this system, because it was seen to be ill adapted to the market economy. As a result of this new "liberal" policy, health care has become a luxury for more and more Chinese people, and a great many underpaid doctors (their salaries are about 500 yuan per month in the cities) don't have their heart in the work. The risk of diagnostic errors and malpractice is correspondingly higher.

"You're not the only one." That was the doctor's only comment to Zhang Qing when she lost her baby during childbirth. The doctor seemed slightly less upset than if he had missed a bus. The dose of anesthetic was probably too high. The young woman launched a malpractice suit against the doctor and won 10,000 yuan in damages after an exhausting court marathon. But the doctor is still practicing, in the same hospital.

City dwellers, many of whom benefit from a minimum of social security, still have the means to take care of themselves in a relatively normal way. But ever since the dismantling of the people's communes, peasants no longer have access to free or low-cost health care. They use the health-care system less and less often and for shorter and shorter periods of time. How many victims of road accidents in the country are dying because the family cannot pay for a hospital visit? How can we explain the disturbing resurgence of respiratory diseases that had been eradicated, except by pointing to the fact that the poorest of the poor do not have the money to consult a doctor and buy medicine?

The Ministry of Health recognizes that the absence of any health insurance system in rural areas leaves 90 percent of the peasants unable to take care of themselves properly. That's 700 million people. Serious illnesses affect 20 to 30 percent of all rural households in the less-developed regions, and infant mortality can reach as high as 70 percent. That's the same rate as in certain African countries that are much poorer than China. In China, money flows like water, sometimes only a dozen miles from the towns and villages where people are living on a few hundred yuan per year. One day in a hospital can cost 100 yuan and an operation 500 yuan—that is, if there's adequate equipment on hand for the operation. Materials are cruelly lacking in the few country hospitals that remain after the dismantling of the people's communes. The inventory of a county clinic serving 20,000 people would look something like this: fewer than ten wooden planks serving as beds, two or three rusty delivery tables, a few shaky stools. No X-ray machine, no laboratory. And a handful of doctors paid peanuts: 250 yuan a month on average, when they're paid at all.

Patients and doctors, professors and students, they're all running wild, rushing to join in the quest for money. The intellectual Yao sometimes takes his chances on a lottery ticket—you never know, it might be his lucky day. What, the lottery in Communist China? Isn't gambling illegal? Officially, it still is. But in 1987 the government granted permission for lotteries to operate on the condition that the revenue be used for charity or sports events and that the prizes be in kind. The games are supervised by the People's Bank of China, the central bank. The fad was so popular that hundreds of towns organized their own lotteries, and the takings did not go into the coffers of the state. As a result, the government had to adopt stricter rules, including prison terms for the organizers of illegal lotteries. In 1995, legal lottery ticket sales rose to 5.5 billion yuan as compared to 2 billion in 1994. Printing presses managed to print 500 million tickets per month although the demand was twice as high.

In 1996, China went into high gear, moving closer to Western lottery operations by introducing tickets that you scratch to win instantly and a televised lotto inspired by the game known in France as Millionaire. The launching of this new game in Liuzhou, in the southern province of Guangxi, was a roaring success. Just think, a gold mine of 100,000 yuan for the lucky winners. The first two grand-prize winners were an unemployed person and a soldier. What great publicity. The authorities defend themselves against the charge of institutionalizing capitalist-style lotteries by pointing out that half the revenue is earmarked for social projects, the other half for the winners. They're "civilized lotteries"—that is, "not rigged." The new tickets are impossible to counterfeit, the sales outlets many and fixed. In theory, that should put an end to the noisy and anarchic lotteries where the grand prizes displayed on stage were somehow never won by anyone. Such con games often led to brawls between duped players and organizers—corrupt Communist officials. Party members know that belonging to the organization that has led the country without any rival since 1949 no longer grants them the same privileges that it used to. Still, they try not to come in last in the race. They don't want to lose face.

Zhang Donghua is certainly right. The Party card, even if it can still open some doors, isn't worth as much as the credit card. Ideally, one should have both.

PARTY OFFICIALS GET DOWN TO BUSINESS

Corruption, in the last few years, has become a new religion in China, bringing together millions of followers rising from the Party ranks. Zhang knows something about this. How many times, at how many levels, has he had to grease the palm of some civil servant? "In China, you cannot get rich legally. The dirty tricks are part of the business," he says. Vigorously denounced by the Beijing Spring demonstrators in 1989, corruption has since gotten even worse, in spite of the launching in 1993 of a big "campaign for a clean government," aimed at calming popular discontent. Heads rolled. The courts came down heavily on those responsible for economic crimes. Hundreds of people were condemned to death and executed for embezzling public funds and accepting bribes. But, with very few exceptions, the guilty who were punished were not in high-ranking positions in the Party. And this crackdown did not have the expected effects. "The lure of gain is too strong—everyone succumbs. From the humblest civil servant to the minister," Zhang believes.

All of China's big financial scandals of the last few years have implicated Party officials. The principal actor in the most extraordinary affair was Chen Xitong, mayor of Beijing, then secretary of the Party for the capital. His time in power lasted twelve years in all. He was a bureaucrat of the regime and one of the most zealous during the bloody repression of 1989. In hindsight, it's easy to understand why this supposedly virtuous Communist wanted to destroy the protesters of Beijing Spring quickly. These "counter-revolutionaries" had the nerve to denounce the exorbitant privileges granted to the ruling elite and to attack the nepotism that makes it possible for the children of dignitaries to live in luxury at the expense of the masses. Still, it took six years after the Tiananmen Square massacres for Chen to be dismissed (a few days after the suicide of Chen Xitong's protégé, a vice-mayor of the capital, Wang Baosen, who was accused of misappropriation of funds) and twelve years in all for the powers-that-be to make up their minds (inspired more by political squabbling between Party factions than by the desire to make a serious effort to fight corruption) to finish with a man whose corrupt practices had been known to everyone for years. After all, Chen had set up a system that benefited hundreds of officials, friends, and relatives.

In September 1995, in a plenary of a Communist Party meeting, the ex-head of the capital, under house arrest, was finally accused of wasting public funds, leading an unprincipled life, breaking the law, encouraging corruption, and being involved in the economic crimes of Wang Baosen. Dismissed from all of his posts, Chen remained a member of the Communist Party for two more years, and it was not until July 1998 that he was finally sentenced for his crimes. He got sixteen years, although others are executed for lesser crimes in China. Eighteen billion yuan officially disappeared from the coffers of the Beijing municipality during the time when Chen Xitong was in command—a sum equal to the budget of this city of 12 million in 1995. Why such leniency? Many citizens of Beijing and foreign analysts believe that Chen Xitong saved his skin by agreeing to keep quiet about the financial misbehavior of other dignitaries who were still in office.

In a totalitarian country where there is no concept of transparency within state-run institutions, corruption is widespread in the police and justice systems. Some policemen specialize in the "shady-bar" racket. It's a simple idea and not stamped "made in China": It consists of raiding certain girlie bars regularly, writing out fines, arresting a few girls who are immediately released, but never definitively shutting down these establishments. Sometimes the establishments are shut down temporarily. There is some common sense to this scheme, since the police themselves own, either directly or indirectly, numerous bars and nightclubs. So does the People's Liberation Army (PLA), which pursues money with the speed of a cruise missile.

The army manages quite well. It has become an essential cog in the economy, an empire within an empire. To finance its own modernization, it has diversified its activities, producing everything from condoms to rockets, including soap, ice cream, bicycles, computers, and trucks. Officially, two-thirds of its conventional weapons factories have been reconverted entirely or in part to civilian production, with a goal of reaching 80 percent by the year 2000.

Once politically powerful, the PLA today is also economically powerful. It is formidable. The government has to go along with it, give in to its whims. After 1989, the army found itself on the other side from the central government on the issue of the austerity policies that were undertaken to cool the economic machine and lower inflation. The most ironic thing was that rising prices had been one of the rallying points of the student population during Beijing Spring—a movement that was fiercely repressed by the army.

Still, all is not rosy in the three-million-man army. Like most state factories, the factories of the PLA encounter financial difficulties because of managers' poor understanding of the workings of the market and their lack of knowledge of consumer expectations. But, with the strength that comes from its influence, the army does not hesitate to expand its activities so that it will come out ahead. Take the example of the Polytechnology arms group, one of the largest in the country. Polytechnology owns the most modern theater in Beijing, Poly Plaza, which stages the most avant-garde performances and the most daring fashion shows. Ticket prices range from 100 to 150 yuan on average, the monthly pay of a soldier at the beginning of his career. The high point of the Poly Plaza's program in recent years was undoubtedly the 1996 show, the first show ever dedicated entirely to modern dance in China. The choreography was perfumed with eroticism. The show was directed and interpreted by the dancer Jing Xin, a transsexual well-known in Beijing artistic circles who (truth is stranger than fiction) started out in an army troupe when she was a young man.

Aware of the key role they play in maintaining the power of the Communist Party, army officers feel no shame rolling down the streets at the wheels of their magnificent foreign limousines. If their modern conveyances tend to blend with the nouveau-riche mass in the cities, they make quite a spectacle on small country roads. When you see gleaming race cars cut across rice fields, ignoring the rules of the road and the safety of the locals, you can bet they belong to the army. You can tell by the special license plates. On the other hand, there's a healthy commerce going in military license plates. It's not unusual for the cars of the new middle class to feature this "option," which costs several thousand yuan—a mere trifle for any limousine owner.

Those who win the prize in the "above the law" category are perhaps the officers of the armed police, a branch of the PLA that plays the role of the Praetorian guard. They love to take their little families out for a Sunday spin, stepping hard on the gas pedal. Nasty clouds of dust fall on the ragged peasants sitting by the side of the road, waiting for God knows what. Maybe for a bus that will take them into the city, where they, in turn, can get rich, like Deng Xiaoping said.

THE BEGGAR'S REVOLT

"Peanut harvest over. Arrive Beijing Monday." Sun Lin had to ask the woman at the post office to help her write the telegram to her future employer. Excitement had robbed Sun Lin of her limited writing ability. The young peasant woman from Henan Province in central China had left school at the age of twelve. "My parents didn't want me to waste my time learning stuff that I'd never end up using. They thought they'd be needing me to cultivate the plot of land they'd just been allotted."

Now, at twenty-one, Sun Lin was on her way to Beijing. In three days, for the first time in her life, this round-faced diminutive woman (five feet tall, 105 pounds), would be in the capital of the People's Republic of China, the Middle Kingdom, the center of the world. Beijing! Tiananmen Square! It was there, on October 1, 1949, that Mao had proclaimed the birth of a new China, a marvelous country where poverty, feudalism, and servitude would be cast forever onto the dust-heap of history, a country in which men and women would be equal, thanks to the Communist Party and the Great Helmsman.

Sun Lin knew the newsreel of October 1 by heart. She had seen it over and over again, thanks to the "barefoot movie projectionists" who traveled around the country entertaining and "educating" the peasantry. She used to love those outdoor evenings when all of the villagers would congregate and sit on minuscule wooden stools normally used by women cooking or by men playing cards. When the People's Cinema was in town the children could stay up late without asking, old people could indulge in interminable conversations about the advantages and disadvantages of decollectivization, and young people could flirt discreetly. Sun Lin and her future husband had taken advantage of movie nights to get to know each other before convincing respective parents to agree to their marriage. At each event, the lovebirds would cross their fingers hoping that the film would snap or the electrical generator would go on the blink, so that they could glean a few extra minutes. The barefoot projectionists have since gone out of circulation. Rumor has it that they now refuse to do such strenuous and poorly paid work, and that a handful have opened a video store in town and are renting pornographic cassettes under the table. In fact, with the gradual spread of television in the countryside, the need for the People's Cinema was bound to disappear eventually. Too bad for lovers.

Sun Lin could care less about the lack of movies in her village. Soon she'd be going out to the movies in Beijing, watching films on giant screens in theaters safe from dust, rain, and wind; theaters where you could eat ice cream. She had seen Beijing's theaters on one of the black-and-white televisions in her village, along with many other fascinating things—notably, how Beijing women dressed and made themselves up. "They must make a fortune," Sun Lin imagined. To her, many of these elegant women closely resembled city women from before the Revolution. Some looked like real women of the world, others like women of little virtue who reminded her of the mistresses of the treacherous and cruel *compredores* who fought against the heroic Party activists in movies. "Oh well," Sun Lin said to herself, "if the Party lets them dress that way, it can't be that bad."

She herself didn't have many clothes. There wasn't much in the big multicolored jute bag that she was taking to Beijing. Her mother had forced her to buy a wool sweater, cotton stretch pants, and a padded jacket so she could look presentable for her employer. If necessary she would complete her wardrobe after she got her first paycheck.

Her first train left at 5 P.M. from Luohe station. To get there she had to take a bus that shook with convulsions, carrying twice the number of passengers permitted by the regulations. Five hours to travel the 93 miles that separated this little city from her village of Yangbu in the south of the province, in a poor region bordered by the Anhui. From Luohe, the local would take her to the provincial capital of Zhengzhou, where she had to transfer to the Beijing express. If all went well, she would be in the capital Monday at dawn. Zhenghou-Beijing: twenty hours in a crammed train making all local stops, sitting on a "hard seat" made out of wood; in newer cars the seats are covered with a thin plastic-covered padding. But Sun Lin could not treat herself to a "hard sleeper," the equivalent of second class, let alone a "soft sleeper," the class for foreigners and professional people. Although it may seem surprising given their profoundly antidemocratic nature, these three classes of the Chinese railway are not an invention of the liberal Deng but of the Communist Mao.

At least Sun Lin had a prepaid ticket guaranteeing her a seat. Not all passengers are so lucky. At each station stop there are terrifying scenes involving hordes of furious peasants who would rather die than miss the train to the promised land. Like Sun Lin, they want to work in the city. The rural exodus is particularly massive in this region. Arable land is getting scarce, and the people are teeming and restless. During the era of the people's communes in the 1960s, the standard of living was low for everyone, and the central activity of each peasant was to work a few hours a day to ensure that there was food for him- or herself and for the collective. One for all and all for one. The rest of his time was divided between the study of Mao's thought and... the study of Mao's thought. Quite a program—although it was never applied as strictly as legend would have it.

The rural scene has been radically transformed by the decollectivization Deng Xiaoping ordered at the beginning of the 1980s, which was intended to establish market value for agricultural products and facilitate the accumulation of individual wealth. Millions of peasants won the jackpot, especially in those provinces where natural conditions were the most favorable. At the same time, the return to private enterprise meant that extra laborers could not just fold their arms as in the times of Mao.

"After the euphoria that succeeded decollectivization, my relatives realized that they were too numerous to cultivate the land. The price of fertilizer was rising, taxes were rising, everything was rising. There had to be some other solution," Sun explains.

Since agricultural resources are limited, the fate of the countryside now depends on industrialization and possibly tourism. And, of course, on the capacity of the peasants to transform themselves. In villages like Beishankou, in the north of Henan Province, with a population of 4,000 souls, there is no longer any distinction between peasants and workers. Here, on the arid hillsides, less then 10 percent of the land is arable, and the rare plots of corn and wheat are intensely cultivated. The obvious solution is for the men to work in the little factories and quarries of the county. The cleverest were those people who started making the transition the soonest. Zhao Kionglin became a blacksmith after he ruined his health for years working as a farmer, trying to make the most out of the semi-desert slopes of his village. In 1993, this man in his sixties with four people working for him had saved 50,000 yuan. "In 1983, I made 85 yuan from the commune," he remembers, with a satisfied but unpretentious smile.

A few kilometers from Beishankou stands the village of Zhulin, touted by local authorities as a model of conversion. These are different times, different mores: In the 1960s, the example to follow was the Dazhai commune with its peasant brigades. Extreme in its mode of operation, Dazhai was an exception. Zhulin is too, in this province where 90 percent of the population lives in the countryside. The average revenue in Zhulin has increased twentyfold in ten years to reach 2,000 yuan in 1992. This is high for Henan, where more than 8 million peasants live at the poverty level with less than 300 yuan per year. The province was not spared the uprisings that spread throughout China in the spring of 1993 in protest against the fall in the standard of living that resulted from the astronomical rise in taxes and farmers being paid in vouchers instead of cash for meager harvests. The remarkable performance of Zhulin is due to the creation of an industrial mini-zone and the establishment of about thirty diverse businesses which receive generous tax breaks from local leaders. "Twenty years ago, we lived like barbarians and ate corn patties every day," remembers a factory director in this village of eighty cars.

Shaolin is also in Henan Province. There, Buddhist monks and heads of martial-arts schools are VIPs. They are not driving around in cars yet, but they may be soon at the rate money is pouring into the birthplace of kung-fu (*wushu* in Chinese). At the beginning of the 1980s, this place was a tranquil village, because Shaolin was not on the list of cities open to foreigners. Visitors could sleep at Dengfeng, the county capital, but only if they had special authorization from the police; their tour of Shaolin had to take place during the day. Finally the monks of the famous temple, the peasants, and the local authorities woke up to the manna presented by the commercial exploitation of the site immortalized in the kung-fu cult film *The Temple of Shaolin*.

Today, Dengfeng County has dozens of schools that educate young people from China and the rest of the world (at different fee scales). The temple also takes in interns in exchange for cash. The largest school, that of the grand master Liu Baoshan, had 2,000 children and 70 instructors at the end of 1994. It's a regular factory, impeccably run by the Liu family who are said to have become the richest family in the area.

It was in Shaolin that the Indian monk Bodhidharma founded his famous meditation school, from which Japanese Zen is derived. Bodhidharma required total stillness from his followers. The legend says that the monk stayed seated before a wall for nine years. To free their discipline from the fetters of immobility, the monks gradually developed a series of movements that eventually evolved into Shaolin boxing. The current inhabitants of the village at the foot of the Song Mountains are breaking out of another sort of immobility—forty years of a planned economy—and leaping nimbly into the new gymnastics of the market.

All over China, villages are changing and peasants are getting rich. The metamorphosis of the less isolated villages in only a few years is remarkable. But most Chinese peasants are not lucky enough to live in a village with touristic or industrial potential. Not everyone can become a blacksmith, *wushu* teacher, or monk! For many, the only answer is to leave the village of their birth. The crumbling of the people's communes has thrown 100 million peasants out onto the streets. At least as many are without work, and, according to the government, 120 million have managed to find jobs in rural businesses of an industrial or commercial nature. Armies of emigrants from poor provinces in the interior continue to drift toward coastal regions and big, thriving cities like Beijing, Shanghai, and Canton, but also to middle-sized cities when the big cities become saturated.

It was Sun Lin's first journey. Gu Jian, her husband, had settled in Beijing six months earlier and had found work as a guard at a security company. She would have liked to have joined him sooner, but she had just given birth to her first child, a girl. Sun Lin waited until the newborn was weaned before packing her bags for Beijing. She had no time to waste. Time is money in year 2000 China. Why hang around your village? Your parents, siblings, and in-laws have more than enough hands to cultivate a few plots of land and raise some pigs and poultry.

Sun's and Gu's parents were not resigned to their dreary life. Somehow they would take matters into their own hands. They were trying to decide whether to open a grocery store or a restaurant in a neighboring town or a taxi company servicing the villages of the area. They would start with just one car. Gu would learn to drive in Beijing. Every evening they talked and talked, cooking up new schemes.

When Sun Lin got the letter from her husband announcing that he had found her a place as a cleaning lady for an old woman in Beijing, she couldn't hold back her tears of joy. In two, three, or at the most five years, she would return to the village with her husband, their pockets full of yuan. They would have a second child, a boy this time for sure. And they would "take the plunge."

The bus trip and the first train trip turned out to be less strenuous than Sun Lin had imagined. She was lucky; on both trips she was seated on two-person benches holding only three passengers. She was no longer in the grip of her earlier excitement, and the sadness of leaving her region and her baby had not yet hit her. Numbly, with fixed eyes, she watched the countryside roll by as if she were watching a movie that had nothing to do with her: outside huge numbers of peasants were doing nothing, playing cards and watching the bus pass by; children were working in the fields; children were on their way to school, running across the fields.

The trip from Zhengzhou to Beijing was more difficult. On three occasions, there were riots when peasants without tickets tried to force themselves onto the train. These incidents delayed the journey for two hours. In one station, the police, armed with electric clubs, struck out at the crowd. Passengers, leaning out the windows of the train, beat back the peasants by hitting them violently on the head with suitcases and metal cups. Ironically, most of the members of law enforcement had been peasants themselves before becoming policemen.

The experience of traveling on the Chinese railway network becomes even more dramatic and explosive during the Lunar New Year holidays, when most migrant workers try to return home. Once you add the civil servants working far from home, the students, professors, and tourists, the number of passengers rises to 150 million. A lively time is had by all.

Day was dawning as the olive green train approached the suburbs of the capital. Sun Lin had not had much sleep. A group of peasants, stinking of cheap sorghum liquor, had spent the night playing cards and yelling. The stops had been very frequent, and very abrupt; whenever the train pulled into a station, it seemed as if the locomotive was braking desperately to avoid some obstacle. That morning the passengers awoke to the sound of a traditional military march blasting out of nasal loudspeakers. Once they had recovered from that assault, they were granted the privilege of hearing a suave feminine voice introduce the capital in a very FM-radio tone, accompanied by a cheerful tune, while the cleaning staff of the train, rags in hand, wiped down the corridors and under the seats. "Beijing is the capital of our country, the People's Republic of China. It was at Beijing on the first of October 1949 that Chairman Mao…"

Sun Lin wasn't listening. Her nose pressed against the window, she was trying to wipe off the filthy pane so she could get a look at the metropolis of her dreams. She saw neither Tiananmen Square, nor the Forbidden City, nor the Temple of the Sky. Instead there were high buildings, cranes, and construction sites. Fleets of cars crawled along as if they were hooked together. Several times she saw a giant yellow letter *M* hanging on a gray building. Sun Lin did not know the whole Roman alphabet but the size of the insignia helped her to recognize the letter. She remembered that her teacher had taught her to write *Mao* and *Marx* in pinyin, the mode of alphabetic transcription adopted by the Chinese in the 1970s.

She would learn later that this mysterious *M* refers to a restaurant that young people like enormously, where you eat a piece of meat between two slices of bread with weirdly sliced potatoes dipped in sweet tomato sauce.

THE LIGHTS OF THE BIG CITY

When she got off the train on March 16, 1994, Sun Lin had a hard time finding her husband. The clamor was terrifying for someone who had never set foot in a city. Braving the tempest of sand and dust that characterizes Beijing at the beginning of spring, the arriving passengers milled around anxiously, mixing with departing passengers, people meeting relatives and friends, as well as the insistent hotel touts, savage taxi drivers, and crooks and con men who, in every country in the world, thrive in train stations full of disoriented people.

The Beijing train station is an imposing yellow building in the Stalinist-Chinese style. Peasants sit and lie in every possible position, awaiting the train that will take them home or to another city—another promised land. The waiting is interminable. Getting a train ticket is quite a feat when one has nobody, when one is nobody. In Beijing, they call the peasants *tu laomao*—"dirt butts." The rural emigrants include many itinerants who try to make a living traveling across the country ten or eleven months out of the year and return to their villages only for the New Year's festivals. If you look closely at the expressions on their faces, you can tell who is going to make it and who is going to struggle—or fail.

Sun Lin's first few days working at Mrs. Chen's were difficult. Not that the ex-business woman was authoritarian. Sun knew very well that she was lucky to be working for this woman, who was perhaps a bit stern but quite nice to Sun Lin considering that most city people had a scornful attitude toward peasants. But it took a bit of time for the Henan peasant to get a handle on things. Work habits turned out to be different in the city than in the country. As a new maid Sun Lin had to learn to use the washing machine, vacuum cleaner, and the toilet. She also had to wash her hands more often than she was used to. Her new boss insisted on it. "How can you wash the dishes if your hands are filthy?" the old lady kept saying.

The vacuum cleaner gave the new cleaning lady endless anxiety. The noise terrified her at first, and she was always afraid that she would accidentally vacuum up other things besides dirt—like the extraordinary collection of Mao badges that Mrs. Chen loved so much. Mrs. Chen had brought the badges out from storage specially for the centennial of the birth of the Great Helmsman in December 1993.

Pleased by their decorative effect, the elderly lady had decided to leave them out in preparation for the twentieth anniversary of the death of the founder of Communist China in 1996.

Sun also had to learn to hold her own with the vendors in the free markets in the neighborhood. The merchants were peasants like her, but they had an irritating tendency to skimp on the weight or to make errors in the adding up. Some had even tried to get her to submit false bills to her employer, in exchange for a percentage of the profits. "All the maids do it," one jovial vendor announced. "What a crazy world I'm in," Sun Lin thought. "Loud, with people running about every which way, ignoring each other except to hurt each other." That's what the city looked like to Sun Lin when she was depressed.

Through Gu Jian, her husband, Sun Lin got a deeper look into this mysterious jungle. Gu was the night watchman in the neighborhood shopping center of Xidan, in the heart of Beijing. He spent part of his days in a sordid dormitory, rented by someone from his county, where he dozed and played cards and mah-jongg—for money—with his "countrymen." Many rural immigrants, upon arriving in the capital, are taken in hand by people from the same province or, better still, the same county. At this level, solidarity still exists. The grouping of peasants by province has given birth to "villages." For a long time, the most well-known of the "villages" was Zhejiang. Located in the southwest part of the city of Beijing, it was a veritable city within a city, housing tens of thousands of newcomers. They were not just peasants looking for any work they could find; among them were tailors and button makers, traditional craftspeople of the region of Wenzhou. Zheijiang quickly became the main supplier of clothes to Beijing markets. At the end of 1995, the municipal government decided to raze the area to satisfy the real estate executives. The news created a stir among the "floating population" of the capital, but it didn't upset the rest of the people of Beijing, who would be up in arms if they themselves were threatened with expulsion. The indifference of the local residents is an indication of their lack of esteem for the emigrants, no matter where they are from. The longtime residents accuse the newcomers of all possible evils, and their arguments are supported by the press. The newspapers cater to the needs of the powers-that-be, who are overwhelmed by social problems and always on the lookout for scapegoats.

"Polls" (the famous polls of the Communist Party) quoted in the papers claim that 70 percent of all crimes are committed by emigrants. The *tu laomao* are also supposedly responsible for spreading microbes and diseases. They are even blamed for traffic jams! Burdened with this reputation, the newcomers are rejected by the more established local population who don't dare set foot in the emigrants' "cut-throat" villages.

Of course, the presence of large numbers of uprooted rural people in cities—in Beijing, they make up one quarter of the population—does pose new social problems. Thugs (from both the city and the country) take advantage of the chaos. The authorities seem to be more interested in finding ways to exploit the situation both politically and financially than in resolving it. Even if they wanted to, it is not clear exactly how they would go about resolving the problems. They have tried ordering the regions to stop handing out travel permits to candidates for the rural exodus. The political leaders of overpopulated provinces didn't see the point of such initiatives. Policemen and Party officials live well off the illegal floating population, taking bribes and selling emigration permits and residence permits at a high price.

Because the government refuses to implement a policy to integrate the peasants into the urban fabric, the most radical strategy it could adopt would be to chase away those who are not really useful. But others would come, attracted by the lights of the big city. The impotence of the authorities will have disastrous social consequences come the day when economic growth decreases and the cities can no longer offer sufficient work to the rural people.

Already clouds are gathering in the clear skies of the economy: Almost one urban resident out of two in the central and western regions has seen his or her buying power fall in 1994 compared with 1993, according to a relatively confidential official Chinese study. And the World Bank estimated at the end of 1996 that the number of people living under the poverty level was 300 million (and not less than 100 million as the government claimed).

THE GAP WIDENS

As economic liberalism progresses, it is clear that income disparities are increasing between regions and between individuals. The rich are getting richer and the poor, poorer. This is a painful social rift for the Chinese and a danger for the future of this vast and populous country.

Salaries in the developed provinces of the east are half again as high as those in the center and west. There are also gaps within each province. A study conducted in 1994 in Jiangsu Province in the east, then ranked tenth out of thirty in terms of development, showed that almost 100 percent of those living in the southern part of the province enjoyed an acceptable standard of living (what the Chinese government calls *xiaokiang*, or "relative prosperity"). In the center of the province the figure was 90 percent, and in the north it was 72 percent.

Within a given city enormous disparities exist. In Shenzhen, the oldest special economic zone, some workers make more than 3,000 yuan and others less than 300. When they have exhausted all of their survival plans and are still floundering, how long will these tens of millions of unfortunate people tolerate the situation? Even the average Chinese person is starting to get worried. The rosy optimism that prevailed in 1992 after the acceleration of reforms is starting to fade. Most people think that their standard of living will continue to improve in the years to come, but more and more fear the contrary. Particularly worried are state employees who fear losing their jobs and old people whose pensions are increasing at a rate slower than that of inflation.

There has never been "one China." But divisions have never been greater than at the end of the century. The only thing everyone has in common is their pursuit of money. It's a race with 1.2 billion participants. Some are sprinting; others are running a marathon that they may never finish, considering the fiendish pace they have set for themselves. The Communist regime knows that it must accomplish at least one thing: raise the standard of living for everyone. When Deng launched economic reforms, he deemed it necessary to allow a small number of Chinese people to get rich first. They would be the locomotive that would pull the rest of the train. Many Chinese are now asking: How long do we have to wait before all of us can get on that train, and maybe even get a seat?

The rapid development of less prosperous regions seems advisable if China is to avoid an implosion set off by social inequalities. With this in mind, the government is trying to reshape the economic landscape, encouraging Chinese and foreign businesses to explore "the Far West." But so far these companies have not exhausted the profits to be made in regions that are more easily accessible. Why should they invest in the end of the world?

For the moment, the rural exodus continues. The despised country folk are in fact indispensable to the city and the government. Almost all construction workers are peasants, and God knows that the Chinese metropolises are growing. Without migration, the building sector could never have taken off. Without the influx of country people, the new middle class wouldn't have maids to clean their houses and babysitters to take care of their children. The people of Beijing and Shanghai have no scruples when it comes to exploiting the peasants. Neither does the state, on construction sites or in workshops. Earning salaries that are half the average, the worker-peasants usually live in shantytowns that are badly heated or not heated at all. They have no work contracts, no social security, and no protection against the many accidents that can happen in the promised land.

Year by year the number of industrial accidents has been rising dramatically. The rusty metal signs preaching in big red ideograms

SECURITY FIRST aren't enough to prevent catastrophes on construction sites. Profit, profit... Every time a tragedy occurs, the authorities are outraged and launch massive inspection campaigns in the city and the surrounding region. The Party leaders give moving tributes to the victims and announce stringent measures for reinforcing security and severe punishments for those responsible for breaking the rules. These politicos are old hands at making promises. Minor work accidents are frequent and are passed over in silence. But neither scorn nor danger discourages the peasants. They have decided at whatever cost to amass enough money for their families to live decently. In any case, back home, there's nothing to do—or very little.

Their backs against the wall, the rural emigrants are ready to fight physically if need be to defend their jobs and their dignity. Tensions between local people and emigrants sometimes turn into bloody confrontations. One of the most deadly occurred near Shenzhen on December 3, 1995. Shenzhen is a symbolic site; it's known as the laboratory of Chinese capitalism. It was there that Deng Xiaoping, on his famous tour in 1992, fired up the leaders and populace to step on the economic accelerator. The drama started with an altercation between a group of emigrants repairing a road and a local who, according to the road workers, drove his motorcycle onto the still-hot asphalt. An attempt to settle the situation rapidly degenerated into a fight. Badly beaten up, the motorcyclist went for help to the town militia and asked them to teach the "dirt-butts" a lesson. After this round, it was the emigrants' turn to mobilize their troops: Fifty or so peasants gathered from the neighboring province of Hunan, Mao's birthplace. They attacked the town, making a point of sacking the Communist Party headquarters with picks and shovels. At last! They spat out their hate, so long contained, toward the authoritarian and corrupt power structure. Then came slow but thorough retribution by the armed police. Rifle shots, rounds of machine-gun fire... The official figures recorded four dead, the unofficial figures, ten. The Chinese press didn't breathe a word about all this, although the tragedy revealed the tense relations between natives and emigrants, the inability of the forces of law and order to handle things, and the extent of lower-class hatred against the regime.

ANY JOB IN THE WORLD

Little by little, Sun Lin realized that although it was indeed possible to build up a small nest egg by slaving away in the city, emigrant life was not the paradise she had imagined. Every morning, on the way to the market, she saw the same group of men sitting at the Dongzhimen crossroads. At their feet were little wooden signs, awkwardly written, specifying their professions: "painter," "tile layer," "carpenter." There are job seekers like this in every city, lined up sometimes for hundreds of feet. One day when the Dongzhimen unemployed were joking away at the top of their voices, Sun Lin recognized the dialect of a county neighboring her own. That's how she met Lao Wu, who had left Henan Province six years earlier, first for Shanghai, like half the men of his village, then for Beijing. Sun and Lao got to know each other, and the unemployed man told Sun Lin his story: "Shanghai was good at first. I made up to 15 yuan a day at the beginning, then there was too much competition and we came up to Beijing." In his village he had to support his wife and three children on 3 yuan per day. "In Beijing you can make up to 40, but now there is too much competition here too."

When he met Sun Lin, he had not worked for two months. This bad stretch had cost him dearly with the owner of the room (ten square meters) that he was sharing with two companions. Lao Wu didn't have the rent money, and his landlord was threatening to send thugs to force him to pay up. In Beijing there are thieves who specialize in attacking people and stealing their hard-earned savings and working in protection rackets targeting illegal emigrants whom they threaten to denounce to the police. Some gangs force emigrants to work for them in order to get their stolen money back. To avoid such problems, Lao Wu never kept any money in Beijing; instead he regularly sent money orders back to his family. He himself said he wanted to go back to Henan in less than ten years, when his children would be big enough to support the family. His sidekick, single and five years younger, was less optimistic. "Maybe I'll end my days here."

Many who came from their "country" with experience as carpenters switched to washing cars. In the absence of garages equipped with automatic car-wash machinery, manual car washing is a business sector that is expanding rapidly. The automobile boom has been a godsend for the unemployed looking for any work whatsoever. There is no residential neighborhood in any big metropolis in China without its squad of men and women rubbing and shining and wiping down cars.

Ai Qing is one of these devoted followers of the religion of automobile cleanliness in Beijing. Morning to night, this young boy from the neighboring province of Hebei stands beside the road in the north of the capital, continually shaking his piece of cloth under the nose of drivers. His spot is near the village of the Olympic Games, a nouveau-riche neighborhood. As soon as one of the cars slows down, Ai Qing sprints to beat out his competitors, hoping that the vehicle will actually stop and that he'll get to wipe off a stain, which will bring him 10 or 20 yuan depending on the type of cleaning involved and the mood of the driver. If the vehicle doesn't stop, Ai Qing has to return to his post very quickly, keeping an eye on the horizon to pinpoint another potential victim. There's no shortage, but he has to keep his eyes open and be quick on the uptake.

The life of street car washers in the north of China is hard: Siberian cold in winter, torrid heat in summer, pollution all year round. "And we have to tolerate abuse from the clients," adds Ai Qing. Nouveau-riche clients are apt to be arrogant and impolite. If only they were a little more generous than the taxi drivers. "Once one guy threw the money on the ground because he said I had scraped his windshield by rubbing too hard," the young peasant remembers. "To humiliate me still more, he threw down twice the normal fee, to show me that I was less than nothing. I bent down and picked up the bills and left without saying anything, letting him savor what he thought was his victory." They call that an "AQ" reaction, "AQ" being the name of a famous character, funny and pathetic, in a novel by the Chinese writer Lu Xun. AQ sees a victory in every defeat. Such a philosophy may help one endure misfortune, but Lu Xun intended his depiction of AQ to be a denunciation of the servile obedience and human cowardice that defined the feudal Confucian system at the beginning of the century. One hundred years and one Communist revolution later, AQ is back on the scene.

Sun Lin is not so different from Ai Qing. She's a disciple of AQ, rolling with the punches, and she's always ready for hard work. For three weeks, she moonlighted as a street vendor. All the other city people work two jobs, why shouldn't she? In the free time her boss left her, she went to her "store"—a spot on the sidewalk. What did she sell? Fruit? Vegetables? No. She sold pirated copies of CDs and CD-ROMs, approaching foreigners in the diplomatic neighborhoods. Fifteen yuan for the CD and 80 yuan for the CD-ROM, five to ten times less than the official price.

She had been recruited by a friend of her husband, who had good connections with the world of counterfeiting. All her colleagues came from the rural suburbs or from the provinces and operated in the same zones or in neighborhood boutiques targeting music-loving Chinese people. Sun Lin had to learn some rudimentary English to address the customers. Her work consisted mainly in pronouncing the magic words: "Seedee Romou, cheepou cheepou, looka looka." Murmured gently and innocently by a smiling young woman, this Anglo-phonetic-Chinese formula could attract the attention of the most reticent passerby. If he allowed himself to be won over and to walk a hundred yards farther on in the steps of his mysterious guide, the customer would discover an Ali Baba's cave piled high with thousands of CDs and CD-ROMs at prices that defied competition—that is, honest competition. These pirated CDs are made in one of thirty or so illegal factories.

American companies believe that this massive pirating hurts their profits, and they insist that the illegal factories be closed down. In an agreement signed between China and the United States in February 1995 to avoid a costly trade war, Beijing committed itself to ending the pirating of audio, video, and computer software products.

Sun Lin was hired to hawk pirated goods almost one year after the conclusion of this compromise agreement. Sincere in its efforts or not, the Chinese government has not been able to put an end to pirating. The practice has continued and even increased, if one is to believe the Americans. In May 1996, a new crisis over pirating broke out between the two countries, Washington accusing Beijing of reneging on its promises. Once again, a compromise was reached. From time to time, to show their good faith, the police and the customs officials in China carry out perfectly orchestrated raids in the presence of official cameras. The invariable scenario—inspection of a store, strong-armed questioning of the personnel, the seizing of merchandise (close-up on the cargo, zoom back, zoom forward, another close-up...), destruction of the pirated products by bulldozer or flamethrower—is designed to impress, and it does. After seeing a TV news report showing salesmen in handcuffs, Sun Lin decided to stop moonlighting as a vendor of pirated goods, for fear of being sent back forcibly to her province. She had made only 100 yuan so far, but she knew that in her country repression always falls on the weak.

For rural people from Fujian Province in the southeast, across from the island of Taiwan, the promised land across national boundaries beckons. These people aim high. Their goal is America, and has been for generations. The economic explosion in their own country hasn't changed this tradition. They are not worse off than others elsewhere, maybe even a bit better off since they live in a province where development is going along well. But they're still hopelessly attracted to Uncle Sam.

Ling Chaoqing, an electrical worker in Banye, a little village in the port community of Changle, used to dream of the United States.

Stubborn, he finally managed to spend almost a year in Los Angeles. "But I never got to see California," jokes this forty-year-old father of three, between two greedy puffs on his black-market Marlboro Light. "Nothing at all, I saw nothing at all," he repeats setting off gales of laughter from members of his family who know the whole story. The Taiwanese cargo vessel on which he stowed away for forty days was intercepted by the U.S. Coast Guard. Placed in a detention center for illegal immigrants, Ling was finally expelled in spite of his repeated attempts to obtain a residence permit in the United States. "I had given 1,000 dollars to a Chinese intermediary and I had promised that once I arrived I would pay 20,000 dollars to the organizers over time," he explains, sitting cross-legged on the ground in front of his family's wooden house from which emanate odors of sticky rice cooked in coconut leaves. "We ate well in the detention center. It was clean and we watched television. But it wasn't California."

There are tens of millions who take their chances on an American adventure. Others try Japan or Australia, or even Europe. Nothing seems to dissuade those who want to go—not the new work opportunities in China, not the risk of prison in China or in the United States, not the hope of someday leaving their country legally, not the danger of death. When the U.S. Coast Guard boards a boat for inspection, illegal passengers don't hesitate to jump overboard and head for the American coastline. Others, lacking the means to pay for a trip in the hold, set out in makeshift vessels and risk shipwreck. For those who make it to America, there is the risk of death from illness or exhaustion in a Chinatown where immigrants work like beasts of burden to reimburse their debts. The youngest often have no choice but to end up as hired men for the Chinese mafia, and the women no choice but to go into prostitution. The risk of living (or dying) in agony ought to discourage many people from making the trip—but it doesn't.

"I don't live so badly here, but there I could earn ten times as much and then come back, invest it, and get rich," explains Ling, whose sister and two brothers have been settled in Los Angeles for several years. "One is legal, the others not so much," he adds maliciously. He swears that at his age, over forty, he won't throw himself into a new adventure. "But I'd be more than happy if my children went to the United States. Legally, if possible, but if there's no other way ..."

The traffic in emigrants brings in several billion dollars per year for the Chinese triads, crime organizations that the international police have not been able to suppress. A large number of gangs have made the trade of smuggling emigrants a specialty; it is more profitable and less risky than selling drugs. The job of Interpol and the national police is made that much more difficult because the mafia has more than enough money to buy off the policemen of Fujian or elsewhere to ensure that the police won't prevent the illegal emigrants from embarking. Obviously, if you question the policemen of the coastal zones, they will swear that they have never, but never, ever touched any bribes from the Dragon Heads and their gangs (whose presence in their territory they will, however, admit). Perhaps a few policemen have gone astray here in the past, but they have been punished, the police representatives in Changle claim.

The ambiguous relationship that has always existed between the Communist leadership and the secret societies does not make law enforcement's struggle to be effective against illegal emigration an easy one. Sometimes the government cracks down, sometimes it closes its eyes, and sometimes it collaborates. "We are ready to work with all of the patriots of Hong Kong," declared the Minister of Public Security, Tao Siju, in 1993, offering an unbelievably frank appraisal of the attitude that the Communist regime would go on to adopt toward the Hong Kong triads after the region reverted to China in 1997. Many Western experts dismiss Beijing's promises to stop illegal emigration, arguing that the Communist regime is only too happy to see portions of its enormous population fly away to an unknown and possibly wretched fate. The cynicism of the Chinese police supports this hypothesis. According to the United Nations, there were 22 million

Chinese people officially living abroad in 1970 and more than 35 million in the 1990s. How many unofficially?

Sun Lin has never been attracted by foreign lands. From her home region, no one has gone farther than Beijing or Shanghai. Here in the capital, it's already like another world—another China, more and more powerful, unconcerned about the widening gulf separating it from the rural areas. City people have absolutely no idea of the life many peasants endure, except for what they see on TV programs about the benefits of decollectivization. The government has had to tone down its propaganda about the systematic enrichment of the countryside, for this message is belied by the huge influx of peasants into the cities and the reported slowdown in agricultural production, notably cereal production. While industry and commerce are exploding, agriculture's performance has been mediocre—a worrying situation.

The urban-rural split is becoming more and more striking. From a twenty-first-century metropolis, one can go a few dozen miles and be back in the nineteenth century. Another contrast also strikes many observers: the contrast between urban and rural women. As Sun Lin had noticed watching the village TV, city women and peasant women face remarkably different challenges.

Chapter *Three*

WOMEN'S LOT IN THE NEW ERA

Xiao Bai glanced brightly at her pager, which was buzzing persistently from within her Chanel handbag, sounding the "Ode to Joy." She loves her beeper; it has six melodies to choose from, and she can change melodies whenever she feels like it. Her cellular phone was conspicuously placed on the table in front of her; she snatched it up as confidently as a businesswoman in a popular television series. It was Liang Jin. He ordered her to come meet him immediately, near the Third Ring Road East at the Shunfeng restaurant—one of those luxurious institutions of Cantonese cuisine, decorated about as discreetly as a Christmas tree, where the newly rich gather to savor the most expensive dishes while drinking cognac at 2,000 yuan a bottle.

With no time to waste, Xiao Bai brusquely said good-bye to the friends with whom she had been killing time in the bar of a big international hotel. She let them take care of the bill: eight coffees (the drink for snobs, who snub the traditional tea preferred by country bumpkins), 160 yuan. That's a fifth of the monthly salary of the young waitress. Here, everything's out of proportion. There's no sense of scale. No wonder the Chinese are disoriented.

Mustn't keep Liang Jin waiting. He hates to wait. She knew what was expected from her from the outset, and she freely accepts her status as concubine. Having to indulge the whims of her almost-husband is the downside of her job. "Concubine—it's my status, it's my career. Half-lover, half-servant. But prostitute, no. Those who take me for a whore are wrong. It's totally clear, if I were unfaithful to my husband and he found out about it, he'd skin me alive. I'm not out of my mind. He sometimes beats me—for example, when I'm very late for important meetings."

That day, the beautiful Xiao Bai, second wife of Liang Jin, arrived on time to the great joy of her "husband," who had organized an important business dinner. His concubine had the task of amusing his highbrow guests. Xiao Bai is perfectly accustomed to this kind of routine. She's impeccable in the role of the frivolous and lively socialite.

It was not long after she failed her high school exams that she met Liang, a real estate agent twenty years her senior, married with children. They met in a karaoke that Xiao Bai was frequenting at the time in the hopes of finding a husband. With her cover-girl figure, big almond eyes, and wide laughing mouth with full lips, the stunning Xiao Bai had never really thought about working in the usual sense of the word. Uninterested in her studies, she dreamt of the easy life. She has it now and says that she has no regrets. Of course, it's not always very comfortable to be the eternal "other woman." Besides enduring the slaps of her strict husband, she has to take nasty comments from one-time friends who are jealous of her social ascent. "And the threat of being discarded is always hanging over me," she confided. Still, Xiao Bai enjoys a luxurious apartment, a sports car, and a hefty allowance.

The first few years, she owned nothing because her "husband" wanted to make sure that she would keep up her side of the bargain. Today, the apartment is in her name. She won that key victory without too much pain. And she thinks it's not impossible that someday she'll be wife number one. "I'm not a slave or a prisoner. I know it's hard to believe for lots of people, but I feel that I'm doing something with my life. Idleness is an art that takes a lot of practice," she jokes, adding more seriously, "It's not so easy to live well. You have to seize the right opportunities. When I think about my girlfriends who spend their time running after Western men and falling flat on their faces, I tell myself that I'm incredibly lucky."

The hunt for foreign men is a favorite sport for young Chinese women, who are persuaded that their lives would be better, or at least easier, with a "long nose" (as the Chinese call Westerners). The tedious daily routine for these girls is to ask themselves where they will hunt the next day. In restaurants, bars, and discothèques, and at private parties, big game abounds. But the terrible family and social pressure compelling women to get married before thirty leads some to throw themselves in desperation into the arms of the first fool they meet, as long as he's a foreigner. All too often, the man only wants to quench his exotic sexual fantasies, to treat himself to some low-cost nights of love. In spite of repeated failures, the girls hang on, just in case. Marriage becomes an obsession, a trap. Once they're on this course, it's hard for them to turn back, since going out with foreigners is looked down upon by many Chinese men. When sheer tenacity is rewarded by marriage, disaster follows. Luckily, once out of China, these women generally know how to take care of themselves. They know at least one Chinese person in the country where they end up. It's an incontestable advantage having 1.2 billion countrymen.

Meanwhile, Chinese girls are starting to understand that today's Chinese boys are not the same as their fathers. They're less macho and more tolerant—no worse than foreigners, and sometimes richer. For these girls and their families, the material factor counts a great deal—as much as love. Why not set one's heart on a rich entrepreneur, even if it means becoming his concubine, as Xiao Bai did.

In a country where poverty lurks everywhere and the future is uncertain, the golden life of the concubine attracts more and more young girls who balk at the idea of throwing themselves into years of grueling study or into some random job. Concubines have made a remarkable comeback since the beginning of the 1990s. They are not the same as mistresses, nor are they prostitutes. Their return to the public scene has not been overly shocking for a population that has grown indulgent toward those who succeed in life without stepping on anyone's toes. Certain items in the press have denounced the resurgence of "feudalism" and the immorality of "the old society" so reviled by the Communists, but there has been no general outcry. The Association of Chinese Women, which is dependent on the Communist Party, issued a few critical comments, but on the whole their response has been moderate. Some of the members of the group even thought that there is nothing humiliating or degrading about being a concubine. On the contrary, they said, it proved that women can assert themselves and enjoy a lifestyle superior to that of many men. Go figure!

The new position of Chinese Communists toward beauty contests illustrates perfectly their pragmatism when it comes to the female persuasion. Once termed decadent and bourgeois, these competitions, usually sponsored by big national or foreign firms, now officially symbolize openness and progress. "The Party has never opposed the election of beauty queens, and now mentalities have changed," a Beijing representative explained without batting an eyelash. She was a wholehearted advocate for this kind of event, judging that the association of beauty and intelligence is nothing to censure. It's funny to hear these remarks from the mouth of a woman in her fifties, dressed with discreet elegance and accustomed to the Party line—a woman who spent her youth decked out in dull overalls or equally boring gray pants. "To us, the queens should be beautiful, cultured, modern, and with a high ideological level," adds this militant feminist, without explaining precisely what she means by "ideological level."

For Liu Xiaoming, a young designer and unsuccessful contestant for the first Miss Beijing competition in 1993, these contests make it possible to "shut the traps of those men and women who think that a beautiful head means an empty brain." Liu underlines her point: "To do what I want and to have fun, that's the opposite of sexual discrimination. Chinese women have been deprived of liberty for so long. Don't attack them now that they are trying to take on new challenges, even if they seem like trivial ones."

EMANCIPATION

The resurgence of concubines and beauty contests may seem like trivial phenomena for a society that is facing so many serious problems. But what these developments reveal is the desire of Chinese women to assert themselves. Today there are more possibilities for emancipation than ever before. Chinese women are the first to admit this (although it may upset the diehard Western feminists who are nostalgic for "revolutionary egalitarianism"). Like Chinese men, Chinese women are chasing after money, but they're also racing to prove themselves, to show what they can do. Mao said that women "hold up half the sky," meaning that women are equal to men. Young Chinese women don't bother with theories about sexual equality, no matter what the source. They fight hard to live better. They are overflowing with enthusiasm and freshness. They are changing in a very profound way, mentally and physically. And in many cases, without being motivated by any unhealthy desire for vengeance, they are surpassing the so-called "stronger sex."

Take Wang Guihua. At the end of the 1970s she was a textile worker; now she is the assistant director of a state-owned fashion company. She is satisfied in her work and well paid, like many other women throughout the country. This dynamic, boyish woman remembers her beginnings in the fashion world: "I was recruited as a model by the Ministry of the Textile Industry in 1979. I was working in a factory, and I was chosen only because I was tall. For a girl of my generation, I am an exception—as far as my size, I mean. It was incredible luck, at first, but after that I worked hard to get where I am today."

Financially, the first years were difficult. Wang made a miserable 30 yuan per month. Psychologically, her lot was hard as well. "You couldn't hope to be accepted by society as a fashion model in 1980. Most people despised us. Now most people think well of this profession, which has since been recognized." Wang is now responsible for organizing the biggest fashion shows in the country. She flies all over China and often goes abroad. "I'm a workaholic. I can't stop. When I wake up in the morning and have nothing to do, I make up a task." One indication of her great love for her work is that she waited to have her first child until she was thirty-seven years old. "I had a strong desire to be a mother, but I knew that I couldn't take care of a child properly. It's too bad because you can only have one. My profession was my priority." What about her husband? "He was very understanding. He's great. But he didn't have much choice," she admits. No doubt about it, Chinese women have new opportunities. They can make it—with a bit of luck, of course, and lots of determination.

Wang Xiaolin confirms this in a different way. When she first arrived in Beijing from Manchuria, this obstinate and hardworking young woman survived by means of odd jobs: mason, beer delivery person, waitress … Now she's designing, making, and selling clothes. "It's hard to be a woman who wants to succeed without bowing down to men, but with perseverance, you can do it. People think I'm uneducated because I sell clothes, but so what? I let them think that. They talk about me because I'm not married and I'm over thirty. They say that I must have a problem that makes no man want me. They never imagine that I might be the one who doesn't want a man. I let them talk," she says in a soft voice that never reveals the exceptional force of character that she possesses.

A private entrepreneur, Xiaolin is hundreds of light-years away from the business milieu of high living and wheeling and dealing. She lives in an old house that doubles as her workshop, where she employs young seamstresses to whom she offers decent pay plus room and board. She lives simply. She doesn't go out to restaurants or nightclubs. A humanitarian, Xiaolin donates a significant part of her profits to young destitute artists and poor families in the neighborhood. "I know it may seem strange, but I want to be useful to society. What good does it do to make money if it doesn't make you completely happy?" she says. This young woman is an exception in a society where individualism is practically a dogma. In any case, her success shows that economic liberalism in China provides women with new opportunities for freedom.

In the workplace, women are taking more responsibility than in the past. There have never been so many businesswomen and professional women. They also play a major role in economic development in that they are driving forces in China's rampant consumerism. At home, they often force the men to share housework. The split is still unequal, but the situation has improved somewhat. Young Chinese women stand up for themselves and are less and less likely to be cowed by their husbands. The rising divorce rate, fueled mainly by women who are dissatisfied in their marriages, indicates the change in Chinese women, even if legal separation remains a difficult choice. Another fundamental change that has come about in these last years: Divorced women are meeting with fewer obstacles to remarriage. Society no longer sees them as lepers.

Despite women's rapid progress in many areas, sexual equality, here as elsewhere, remains a goal proclaimed by the authorities but far from achieved. Flagrant discrimination remains in education, salaries, and political responsibilities: Women study for shorter periods of time; they earn less; as yet there is no woman in the politburo of the Communist Party, which is the real government (although this realm doesn't attract lots of women any more than it does men).

Before the World Conference of Women in Beijing in September 1995, the government once again committed itself to improving women's lot in a policy statement that implicitly recognized the relative failure of measures adopted in the past. The goals of equality in political and social life had already been formulated by Mao himself,

in his famous expression about women holding up "half of the sky."
More prudently, the 1995 document announced, "Women still have a
long and difficult path to travel."

TRAGIC DESTINIES

The encouraging success of millions of women should not make us
forget the hard lot of others. Women are often the first victims of the
untrammeled capitalism in China, but no one dares talk about their
fates. Women—and girls. The "little hands of Anhui" are peasant
girls, barely fifteen years old, from Anhui Province, who slave away
in Shanghai or elsewhere in sweatshops owned either privately or by
the state. Child labor violates the work code, the law for the protection of minors, and the International Convention of the Rights of the
Child ratified by China in 1992. The "little hands of Anhui" and millions of other children leave behind their school books on their parents' orders. In the coastal southern provinces, which are the most
dynamic business centers, this cheap and tractable labor pool is
mainly employed in restaurants and businesses. Some state factories
that are in desperate financial straits also exploit children, often
girls, without encountering any special objections from the authorities. The union—the one affiliated with the Communist Party—does-
n't object; the children are helping a state business to stay in business, and that looks good in the statistics. If by some happy chance
the factory takes off again, the children will be politely thanked and
sent on their way, and the management will turn once again to adult
employees, who are better qualified and better paid—that is, until
the next crisis.

It is not only children who suffer in China's new era. Here's the
story of a young woman who will remain nameless. She was too modest, too reticent, to let her name be known. She had come to Beijing
from a middle-sized city in the south of Shandong Province, near the
borders of Anhui, an underdeveloped region. She was sick of working

at a two-star hotel in her city. The city was as ugly and dreary as its inhabitants. She was going nowhere and had promised herself she would make it to the big city. Every night she dreamt about Beijing: the bright lights, the Great Wall, and the great shopping. A thrilling life—a real life. She didn't know exactly what she'd do in Beijing, but in her pockets she had the names of some distant cousins, and in her heart she had determination. She told herself that she was bound to find work in a hotel. Three months after her arrival, still unemployed, the little provincial girl from Shandong was raped and jailed.

Her cousins helped her out at first. Thanks to them, she found a place to live in Haidian, the university neighborhood, not far from where Professor Yao lives. It was a dark little room on the fourth floor of an old building belonging to the municipality. Employees of the national educational system rent apartments there for token sums, and some of them then sublet their apartments illegally for the exorbitant price of 300 yuan per month. The authorities turn a blind eye to this practice. Since the revolt of spring 1989, the government has tried to avoid anything that might cause intellectuals to be any more discontented than they already are. Unable or unwilling to raise salaries too rapidly, the government has no interest in opposing these illegal sublets, which are good for everybody—Beijing citizens and the emigrants.

The Shandong girl agreed to share her little room with a roommate, a certain Zhao, from Henan. Zhao, a clever little schemer, immediately put the young newcomer in touch with the Ma brothers, two petty criminals. In exchange for the few hundred yuan she needed while she waited to land a real job, the peasant girl agreed to hide the loot from their burglaries, promising herself not to turn this somewhat risky business into a permanent thing. One day, when she went to the Ma brothers' place to pick up the latest booty, she found the crooks in an advanced state of inebriation in the company of a girl whose job apparently went beyond hiding stolen objects. The peasant girl will never forget the hell of that afternoon. She was raped. The most painful aspect of her experience, which she still feels today, worse than the wounds in her flesh, was the indifference of the neighbors to her screams and cries for help. In a building where most of the residents are illegal workers, cowardice lives on every floor. See no evil, hear no evil.

At the police station, she found not cowardice, but cruelty. A policeman tried to talk her out of reporting the rape. Finally he wrote up her accusation with about as much enthusiasm as if he were attending a political meeting. Three days later she was arrested for prostitution. The police took her to a local compound full of thieves, homeless people, and prostitutes. She was furious at herself for having dared to lodge the complaint. She had hesitated a long time, out of modesty and fear about being mixed up in activities related to theft.

The police imposed a sentence of twenty days in a reeducation camp. They have the right to make such decisions according to the law on administrative detention. Citizens can be detained for up to three years. She found herself in the women's prison at Changping, in the north of Beijing. It was dirty with overcrowded cells, revolting food, and every illness you can imagine, including AIDS—for China is not immune to the plague.

Take the biggest population in the world, mix well with two tons of sexual taboos, irresponsible authorities, and the race for money, and you'll get one of the most explosive cocktails in the world in terms of the AIDS epidemic. Officially, the HIV-positive in China numbered only 10,000 in March 1998, concentrated for the most part in the southern provinces of Yunnan and Guangxi, key crossroads for the drug traffic in China and Asia. The figure is pure fantasy. Chinese experts estimate the number of people carrying the virus at more than 100,000, and UNAIDS, the United Nations AIDS program, estimates the figure to be 200,000—not surprising figures when you consider the size of the country's population. In the absence of any serious AIDS testing, the government's attempt to hide the truth makes it impossible to get an accurate picture of the situation. In any case, the equation DRUGS = AIDS is not enough to explain the propagation of the virus nor the rise in venereal diseases. Prostitution and the loosening of sexual mores are the deeper root causes.

SEX, LIES, AND PROPAGANDA

Although prostitution is still illegal in China, the sex industry is flourishing—in the city, in the country, in the streets, by the side of the road, in houses of prostitution, in nightclubs, bars, and even state-run hotels. Once reserved for foreigners and superwealthy businessmen, prostitution now attracts a clientele of middle-class Chinese whose higher earnings allow them a few private pleasures. There's something for everyone, at every price. This country once claimed to have eradicated prostitution through "mass education" and "anti-vice campaigns" involving the imprisonment of streetwalkers and the execution of small-time pimps. Now it's the return of the repressed. Money has once again triumphed over politics. The whole country is in danger of paying a very high price for revolutionary frustration. The Chinese mafia has taken upon itself the organization of the sex industry. The secret societies in Hong Kong and on the mainland have made a lot of progress in this area, especially in the southern part of the country where they also control the traffic in drugs and arms. The sex industry pays so well that nothing can prevent its expansion—not even the devastation of AIDS and other sexually transmitted diseases.

May 1996 was right smack in the middle of a national repressive campaign known as *yangda*, "strike hard," which was supposed to scare small-time delinquents and organized gangs and wipe out the revival of the criminal elements. In spite of the announcement of the arrest of thousands of their colleagues, the prostitutes of the autonomous region of Guangxi, just north of Vietnam, didn't seem to feel threatened.

Guilin is a city known throughout the world. Its enchanting countryside of limestone hills is the inevitable cliché of every tourist brochure on China. Along with Hangzhou, near Shanghai, Guilin is the most touristy city in the Middle Kingdom. But there's one street in Guilin that is known to everyone in the city but doesn't appear on any tourist map. It's the "rue de Paris," on the road running north of the city, where foreigners rarely go. For a massage (or a "massage"), customers don't need to go that far: Guilin has as many beauty salons and seedy bars as it has hills. The high cost of entry makes their real purpose clear. The service in the rue de Paris, of course, is cheaper.

This murky thoroughfare with its cracked asphalt is entirely dedicated to the sex industry. On both sides of the street, for about 328 yards, there is nothing but hotels that serve as brothels. These small, recently constructed buildings of three or four stories have ground-floor rooms open to the sidewalk, furnished with sofas and a few tired armchairs covered in cheap leatherette. A few hundred girls work here. They're very young, not very pretty, and badly dressed—they're peasants. Not one of them looks like the classic image of the prostitute. They have neither the charm nor the vulgarity of their counterparts in the city. They barely manage to attract potential clients. In their gaze, there is either lassitude or a pathetic shyness. They're new recruits; probably they've been kidnapped by gangs specializing in procuring women and children, or maybe they were sold by lazy or destitute parents. The trade in women is a profitable business. In poor regions, a young girl can fetch 2,000 yuan.

Who's buying on the rue de Paris? The average guy. Taxi drivers, employees, white-collar workers on business trips who ask for receipts so they can get reimbursed by their companies. Not that the sex they buy costs enough to break them. It's rarely more than 100 yuan, even for love. The simpler acts take place in the back room, on the ground floor, in cubicles sometimes separated only by a filthy curtain. For wilder times, one goes upstairs to minuscule rooms that are cleaned at most once a year for the Spring festival, and that feature repellent bedclothes, cheap lighting, cockroaches, and stench. The pimps are never far away. They're sitting in their offices—the bars or restaurants on the street. Who really runs the rue de Paris? The girls don't have much to say on this subject. The taxi drivers are more loquacious but still vague. "The street's been like that for two or three years. Every one in Guilin knows about it. The cops come by occasionally, but they don't do anything. Some people say that the municipality gets money from the gangs that run the street between them," one of the cabbies says.

Liang Meiling worked for a year on rue de Paris before being hired in a karaoke downtown. "The managers of the massage parlors and clubs of the city go out there regularly to recruit the prettiest girls, and the men on the rue de Paris can't do anything about it. That's how I made the transition. I'm happy, because it was rough. Like lambs to the slaughter. You could never say no to a client. In the karaoke, the clientele is more high-class, looking for a good time without necessarily wanting to make love. And then there's the tips. In a good month, I make more than 5,000 yuan—less than a masseuse, but the work's not as tiring." Liang Meiling does not have terribly ambitious plans. She's happy enough to make a good living. She turns over a major portion of her salary to her parents, both of whom work 31 miles outside of Guilin in factories that aren't doing too well. "My father hasn't been paid for three months. Things are tough all over. With my level of secondary schooling what could I possibly do? In the provincial administration and businesses, there have been layoffs. So, for me, it has to be the private sector. I got into prostitution by accident. I'll get out of it when I feel like it. There'll always be someone else to take my place. But I don't tell everyone I'm a whore. It would bother me. My parents think I'm a waitress."

Every self-respecting tourist who visits Guilin makes the spectacular descent on the Li River to Yangshuo, a little town tucked away in a sumptuous natural environment. The spot is sought after by travelers from all over the world, who come for the hippie atmosphere, the friendliness, the muesli at breakfast, and the long, peaceful days that may be spent wandering through the rice fields and along the banks of the Li River—cut-rate calm and authenticity in a country where ripping off tourists is a national policy. Since the mid-1990s, a paved road joins Yangshuo to the neighboring province of Guangdong. A paved road means trucks, trucks mean truck drivers, and truck drivers mean prostitutes. While the travelers tranquilly sip their last beers before sacking out, listening to Neil Young and Leonard Cohen in cheery, wholesome cafés, truckers cruise to beauty salons and little hotels on the other side of town. The spot reserved for tourist buses during the day is a rallying point during the night for truckers looking for a female passenger. Throughout the country, brothels for truck drivers provide work for young peasant women in poor areas. It seems unlikely that the use of condoms is widespread on the Guangxi roads.

Farther south is Liuzhou, the main industrial center of Guangxi. It's a humdrum city, an economic boomtown, with an average standard of living and only a few wealthy residents, but lots of prostitutes. They're everywhere, even in the hotel run by the Communist municipality. It's the best hotel in town, the one where local political leaders organize meetings and seminars. The lobby is just like that of any other big hotel, with its spic-and-span reception desk and receptionist fitted out in very proper attire. On the walls hang the photos of the top leaders who have stayed there—among others, the president of the Association of Chinese Women, Chen Muhua, well known for her high-powered speeches on socialist morality and her diatribes against Western decadence. Did Mrs. Chen take the time to visit the basement of this hotel with its "amusement center," as advertised in hotel pamphlets? Surely not. Perhaps Mrs. Chen was turned off by its name, the King of Spending. Spending on what? Sauna, massage, bar, classic cocktail lounge. Dozens of girls are turning tricks in the corridor, which is lined with massage booths. You might think that this is all there is to the sex industry in Liuzhou, but you'd be wrong. Liuzhou also has its own rue de Paris, twice as long as the one in Guilin. The sex industry seems to crop up absolutely anywhere—in tourist areas and in the most anonymous of cities. Soon every part of China will have its own rue de Paris and its King of Spending. How many prostitutes will there be then?

In Nanning, capital of Guangxi, the business of soliciting is somewhat more discreet. The same is true in regional political centers, where the authorities care more about protecting the image of the city. Nonetheless, erotic or naughty shows are everywhere, even in certain state hotels. Of course, one shouldn't confuse cabarets with brothels. On the whole, the clientele is different. Those who go to a cabaret looking for a real thrill are going to be disappointed, tricked by the misleading posters of scantily clad girls in suggestive positions. Although cabarets and brothels are not identical twins, they may have the same parents: the mafia.

The very official Palace of Worker's Culture, which for the last forty years presented good-natured circus shows and song-and-dance numbers steeped in socialist realism, has more recently given in to the fever for modernization. It has been transformed by local leaders into an ultrasophisticated entertainment complex designed to host all kinds of shows. On the esplanade stands a magnificent statue of Caesar. The Roman emperor is fashionable in China's nightclub sector—a symbol of grandeur, of debauchery, an invitation to orgy?

Unable, or unwilling, to slow down the lucrative activities of the sex industry, the government will have to speed up its efforts to combat sexually transmitted diseases or face human disaster. In China, sexually transmitted diseases are not identified in time, nor are they treated appropriately. Medically and psychologically, China is even less prepared than are the Western countries to face AIDS. When the first cases were discovered in the United States, Europe, and Africa, the Chinese government preferred to shut its eyes. AIDS was considered a foreigners' disease that could never cross the Great Wall. Why? Because China is a socialist country, the officials of the Department of Contagious Diseases at the Ministry of Health responded. Their wide, complacent, compassionate smiles seemed to say, "Too bad for you Westerners, but then again, you asked for it." In a socialist country, homosexuality, prostitution, extramarital relations, and drug addiction don't exist. Everyone knows that these decadent horrors were swept away by the Red tornado after 1949. The Communists certainly didn't skimp on the resources when it came to getting rid of these scourges, but the same problems reappeared with a vengeance at the beginning of the 1980s, and the government has refused to admit it. To recognize the problem would amount to a confession—another one—of the failure of a policy that, as is always the case in a totalitarian regime, had been proclaimed victorious before it was even put into action.

With the brutal liberalization of the economy, which was necessary to keep the Communist Party in power, this denial has had to stop. Homosexuality, prostitution, cruising, and drugs are no longer taboo subjects, although mention of homosexuality is toned down in the official press. For forty years homosexuality was considered a mental illness. Change is bound to be slow. Many Chinese people still hesitate to speak openly about their sexual problems, in spite of the current "liberation." This attitude does not make the fight against AIDS any easier.

Sexually transmitted diseases are gaining ground, and the authorities don't seem to realize the extent of the danger. As a concession to the medical community, which has a clearer idea of the danger but is itself insufficiently informed to confront these illnesses, the Ministry of Health in the 1990s started a timid educational campaign about the dangers of unprotected sex. On World AIDS Day, December 1, some information is disseminated, mainly on television. All the same, in many documents sexually transmitted diseases are presented as illnesses that are of importance abroad. Such a presentation weakens the impact of messages of prevention. The government does not yet provide the funds necessary to mount an effective struggle against sexually transmitted diseases and tends to depend on international aid. The provinces are expected to cope with these problems themselves. Several research and testing centers have opened, in Beijing and Nanjing in particular. Although the centers have impressive-sounding names, their resources are totally inadequate to meet the needs of the population, and the staff are insufficiently trained. In the southern provinces, the areas most touched by the illness, clinics are besieged every day by hundreds of people who, after having unprotected sex, are infected or are afraid of infection. Condoms are not freely available in most regions; family planning centers are stingy about handing them out.

The Ma brothers didn't use condoms, and the peasant girl they raped had to have a secret abortion after bribing a nurse. With no residence permit and no work, migrants have no access to public health. When the peasant girl got out of prison, she tried to find a legal solution to her problems but gave up after a year or two. Her parents know nothing about this story. They think their daughter is making it in the big city and soon she'll start sending home money. As planned.

Chapter *Four*

THE GOOD LIFE

"The only pamphlets the Chinese have the right to distribute are ads!" Professor Yao, irritated and a little drunk, spat out this phrase in an argument with his brother-in-law about whether the Chinese have more or less freedom today than before 1989. A Party member living in Hubei, a province in central China, his brother-in-law supported the June 4 repression without hesitation, although, like many provincial folk, he had little idea of exactly what had happened in Tiananmen Square before, during, and after that tragic night. He still approves of the government's decision to call out the army to put an end to the revolt, and he justifies his position by citing the economic victories that have been won since—successes that, he claims, were made possible by the stability of the regime.

The two men often quarrel about political matters. Neither one ever budges from his position or gives in on any point. One pleads in favor of Liberty with a capital *L*, the other for Order with a capital *O*. But the two do agree on one important point: Most Chinese live better today than they did before Beijing Spring. All the same, Professor Yao fears that the reign of the money-god will lead to catastrophe.

Meanwhile, the Chinese are taking advantage of the economic boom while they can, and the professor is first among them. They are frantically consuming. Observers in industrialized countries, faced with sluggish sales and dwindling growth at home, cast admiring glances at China.

The Sunday outing of the average Chinese family is not to the Worker's Park but to the department store. Junior heads not for the swing set but for the toy department. He lunches not on ice cream but on hamburgers and french fries from the fast-food restaurant in the shopping center. In the country, peasants walk doggedly for miles, over hill and dale, to shop not in the nearest town but in the one that's best stocked. The powerful attraction of consumption is as irresistible and sudden as a hurricane. The good old state stores called *bai-houdalou* (buildings of a hundred things) have had their day. Farewell to depressing shelves and surly salesgirls. These relics of socialist planning no longer attract anyone but nostalgics, tourists, and peasants who've lost their way. These stores have to adapt if they hope to hold their own against their seductive competitors. Most shoppers in small and big cities prefer the specialized boutiques, supermarkets, and luxury department stores that are popping up all over the country. The high prices at these department stores suggest that they attract more visitors than shoppers, but the magic of their attraction is undeniable.

There has been another big commercial revolution: stores close late. Stores have always been open seven days a week. In China, there's never been any debate about being open on Sundays. Up until 1994, the notion of the weekend didn't exist, and the introduction of the forty-hour workweek hasn't changed life much. Before the economic reforms, the choice of stores was small, as was the amount of cash in the shopper's billfold. Now that consumerism is the favorite hobby of Chinese, there's no store of any kind that would deprive itself of Sunday's receipts. Why close? Do you think the Chinese people are off to Mass? Sunday is hardly the Lord's day in China.

Chinese capitalists are not going to worry about a few million Catholics who might just as well attend religious services Saturday evening or early Sunday morning. The Patriotic Church of China is an institution that is controlled financially and politically by the state. The Church does not recognize papal authority and names its own clergy. The split with the Vatican dates back to 1950 and is both political—because the Communist Party does not want religion to serve as an ideological rival—and diplomatic—because the Holy See keeps up diplomatic relations with Taiwan, the renegade isle that China hopes to recover one day.

Beijing and the Holy See have launched a cautious dialog, but the Communist regime remains firm on the basic principle regarding the limited freedom of Catholics: There is to be no relationship with the Vatican. Officially, there are about 8 million Christians. Unofficially, there are twice that many, if you count those who are faithful to the Pope and who meet clandestinely in the so-called Church of Silence, as well as the unauthorized Protestant groups. The Communist Party, through the associations it finances, also controls all the other major faiths. Thus in Communist China, where the overwhelming majority of the population is atheist, there is no separation of church and state. Muslims and Buddhists are particularly watched by the government, since these faiths have played a role in independence movements in Xinjiang and Tibet.

The first Constitution of the People's Republic guaranteed freedom of religion, but this right was put into practice in a careful, limited way, only in the mid-1980s. In theory, the Constitution allows several tens of millions of people to practice their religion without fear of being persecuted as they were during the Cultural Revolution. Still, believers had better respect the rules of the game as set down by the government. Those who fail to do so risk being sentenced to a prison term in a reeducation camp. According to international human rights organizations, the Communist regime is intensifying efforts to control religious activities. Repression against unauthorized groups and sects has definitely increased in the years following the easing of restrictions at the beginning of the 1980s. Reliable sources attest to detentions, cases of torture, and the destruction of places of worship deemed dangerous to the public order. At the beginning of 1996, the government announced its intention to establish a complete legislative arsenal to be used to prevent religion from being used "against socialism and the unity of the country." Two years earlier, the National People's Congress had adopted two laws reinforcing control over places of worship and the religious practices of foreigners in China.

Religion is no longer called the opiate of the masses—although the concept still appears from time to time in the press—yet the Communist Party fears religion as if it were not a drug but a plague. With great regret, the Party has had to face the fact that with the development of a very materialist society has come the return of the spiritual in full force. In the city, and to an even greater degree in the country, popular religions are openly attracting more and more followers. In many rural regions, religious institutions are becoming veritable alternatives to feeble Party power. There is a notable rise in the numbers of the adherents of all faiths and all ages, and the fervor of the followers is impressive. The religion of consumerism is not enough to fill the ideological vacuum left by the death of Mao. Stores stay full, and so do churches, temples and mosques. The only difference is one of scale.

Of course, places of worship don't benefit from advertising. Advertising everywhere relegates political slogans to the rank of curiosities. The new billboards are a big disappointment to foreign tourists and armchair revolutionaries looking for proletarian novelties: the red banners that brighten the streets have no slogans more "authentic" than DISCOUNT SALE AT WANG'S or SPECIAL ON LIPSTICK. In Xidan, the neighborhood where the dissident Democracy Wall movement took place in 1979, there are no more *dazibao*. Even the wheezing accordion buses and subway trains are plastered with aggressive ads. Welcome to Consumerland!

An essential element of the new consumer society is television, with its ads, made-for-TV films, and sitcoms that look like they were shot in department stores. State grants for TV have been considerably reduced and television now supports itself primarily through advertising. The first Chinese TV ad was a liquor commercial distributed in Shanghai on January 28, 1979, at a time when the country was timidly beginning to talk about a market economy. Since then, commercials have invaded TV. Chinese and foreign businesses bid higher and higher for the time slot just before and after the evening news. Rates rise but it's worth it. Advertisers who get that evening slot report a rise in sales. It's simple: More than 400 million TV viewers turn on their sets for the news. A business that spends 200 million yuan to go on the air just after this cathode-ray Grand Mass is actually paying only 0.5 yuan per viewer. Thus each year 10,000 companies compete to place an ad in the minute between the news and the weather. Ad agencies are rubbing their hands—at least the top agencies are, because competition is rough.

Movie actors and directors are taking advantage of the boom in advertising to bring in a little extra on the side. The most ever made by a movie star for an ad was one million yuan. That's what China's highest-paid movie star, Gong Li, made for an ad for Meide air-conditioning in 1993. The average annual revenue for a Chinese worker that year was 2,000 yuan.

Besides TV ads, there are "consumer awareness" shows, nothing more than infomercials for the products that are "compared," and shopping shows broadcast nationally, regionally, and locally. Chinese viewers can spend several hours a day consuming through the little screen. The official print press, like the *People's Daily*, is not immune to advertising fever. The Shanghai newspaper *Wenhui* inaugurated a new genre on January 25, 1993, by publishing a front page devoted entirely to advertising. The headline was THE HOTTEST SUBJECT OF THE SUMMER WILL BE COLD—an ad for Western Cold air-conditioning. There was not one line of news, not one photo on this historic front page.

This should remind us that Shanghai is the Chinese cradle of Western-style consumerism.

It is hard for the Chinese to ignore the media hysteria. They buy, buy, buy—women and children first. They are the principal motors of consumerism in food, clothes, cosmetics, and, of course, toys. In cities, almost all households are equipped like Western homes: refrigerator, washing machine, hi-fi, television set, and VCR. (In the poorest rural areas, households still have less than 10 percent of the basic household appliances.) Between 1990 and 1995, retail sales in China rose by more than 20 percent per year—in certain major cities, by 35 percent. This hyperconsumerism has contributed to an already-galloping rate of inflation, originally generated by too many investments. But inflation doesn't seem to demoralize consumers; they're enjoying this new freedom to buy. For many of them, spending is a way of meeting needs that are more than just material. The Chinese are entering into the civilization of the superfluous, of pleasure.

Members of the power elite were once the only ones who knew the intoxicating feeling of spending money for things other than rice and soap. Revolutionary leaders dared to preach frugality while shamelessly helping themselves to the goods in the stores reserved for foreigners, the so-called "stores of friendship," known for the impoliteness of the personnel. These socialist supermarkets only accepted strong currency. Today they accept everybody—and everybody's money. They have to. They're faced with competition from shopping centers, small private boutiques, and the noisy colorful markets that vitalize streets that were once bathed in calm. Some people miss the tranquillity that made their neighborhoods so charming. But the new convenience stores, opening early and closing late, are very practical for people who are now more active than they once were, people whose time is now limited. A plethora of little stores and minuscule stalls manage to survive in the midst of vicious competition.

COUNTERFEIT HEAVEN

What's original about the merchandise that is on offer? Does it have a "Chinese character"—to use a phrase that is fashionable in the corridors of power in Beijing? Yes. It's fake. Imitation goods and goods of poor quality account for more than half of all sales. Cheating is everywhere, in every sector. There's fake food, fake medicine, fake clothes, and fake cars. If it's just the brand name that's fake, the alert consumer (and there aren't many) will suffer from nothing worse than wounded pride. In the case of certain foods, the consequences of cheating can be more dangerous. An inquiry by the Ministry of Health in 1996 showed, for example, that three out of four brands of mineral water, five out of ten brands of biscuits, and eight out of seventeen brands of milk were below standard norms of quality and hygiene. Some products were found to be harmful or to contain poisonous substances. Adulterated liquor and fake medicine kill or seriously wound hundreds of people each year in China. Countless Chinese people become blind after drinking what they thought was rice liquor or are struck down after taking pills for intestinal trouble.

To protect consumers, the National People's Congress Parliament adopted a law in 1994 specifying that victims have legal recourse and that offenders would receive specific sentences for breaking the law. The new legislation has not yet wiped out counterfeiting. The practice may well remain widespread, considering the lack of scruples of Chinese manufacturers. Their goal is to get rich quick any way they can, no matter what it entails. On the positive side, because of the abundance of imitation products, a consumers' rights movement has developed, made up of nonprofit associations headed, of course, by Communist Party organizations.

In 1995 one young man decided that these organizations were too timid and launched himself into solo combat against counterfeiters of all kinds. For many Chinese people, this ex-student and maverick seeker of justice, named Wang Hai, merits the title of national hero. For others, he's just another fake, an impostor who has found his own clever way to get rich.

This Chinese Ralph Nader started out buying up dozens of samples of any product he judged to be counterfeit, concentrating on electronic goods with foreign brand names. He went to the real manufacturers, got confirmation of the imitation, and then forced those who were selling the fake merchandise to conform to an article of the consumers' rights law that stipulates that consumers are entitled to double their money back on counterfeit products. Wang's exploits were publicized all over the country, and he became the terror of shopkeepers. He was last seen in Canton! Oh, no, he's popped up again in Shanghai! No sooner had he been tracked down than he was off again, pursuing his crusade in other fertile territory. A persistent but contested rumor has it that Wang has amassed a fortune. Undaunted by his detractors and supported by the press which has always denounced fakery, Wang has continued his struggle. On March 16, 1996, National Consumer's Day, he participated on a TV show. Courageous but not foolhardy, Wang wore a fake moustache and dark glasses, saying he'd received death threats! Was this the real thing or a publicity stunt? The show blew the top off the Beijing channel's ratings, and the station sold lots of good advertising time—but for real or fake products?

Wang has written a book about his memorable experiences (*I Am a Rogue*) and writes a regular consumer column in the *China Youth Daily*. His lone crusade has grown: his Beijing Dahai Commercial Consulting Company now has a well-known consumer hotline and a national network of two hundred informers reporting suspected fakes.

Zhang Donghua is well aware that he buys fake products—fake luxury products, that is. Copies of luxury products, often made in China, flood the world market as well as the local market, from which they sprung. Zhang frequents luxury boutiques exclusively—a man of his standing would lose face if he were seen with a shopping bag from an ordinary store—but it's mainly Zhang's wife who splurges on clothes, shows, household goods, makeup, and so on. She likes to buy both quantity and quality, if possible. Mrs. Zhang is God's gift to the cosmetics industry. In major cities, the average amount women spend on beauty products is 20 percent of their personal budget. The revenue of the cosmetics industry reached 10 billion yuan in 1994 compared to 200 million ten years earlier. Between 1979 and 1995, the number of beauty salons and hairdressers' establishments grew from 10,000 to 700,000. There are as many hairdressers in China as there are cafés in France.

Professor Yao cannot be as extravagant as Mr. and Mrs. Zhang, so he splurges on restaurants rather than on luxury goods. Still, when he does go shopping, he pays prices that he would have found unthinkable a few years ago. Feeling sorry for himself all the while, he nonetheless forks over 100 yuan for a sweater, spending a quarter of his professor's monthly salary and calling it "a bargain."

Sun Lin's first window-shopping expedition in Beijing turned into a nightmare. She felt real terror—a terror as intense as what she had felt when, as a little girl, her grandfather told her horrible tales of the Japanese tracking down Communist resistance fighters in the fields. The resistance fighters—except for the hero—bravely perished after suffering the sophisticated torture of the pitiless soldiers of the Rising Sun.

Sun Lin couldn't believe her eyes. The luxury oozing from the shop windows terrified her. She stood for many long minutes—she couldn't say how long—stock still in front of one of the windows displaying articles of women's clothing costing several thousand yuan. She was surprised to learn that there were women in her country wearing underclothes worth one month of her salary. There were men's suits priced at 3,000 yuan and children's shoes at 200 that made her think of her child. She began to walk more and more quickly, looking behind her over and over again, convinced she was being followed.

That night she had a horrible dream. An army of salesmen and salesladies in uniform, speaking Japanese, were chasing her around a gigantic labyrinthine store. They were brandishing vacuum cleaners and shouting: "Our business will conquer. Death to deserters!" Her husband had been tied up by salespeople who wanted him to confess how much money he had saved....

Sun Lin was out of her element. She never entered the stores that she nicknamed "Nippon blockhouses." But little by little she discovered other department stores, modern enough and less expensive. These stores had strange, garish little commercial presentations, often modeled by hostesses in miniskirts and high heels. At first, the young peasant woman thought these commercial striptease shows were shocking. Then she got used to them, finding that the bare legs of the girls could be beautiful. "But that's not for me, I'd be ashamed to wear that and my husband would kill me." Miniskirts are an indispensable promotional tool in the Middle Kingdom, just as in another era the Mao suit helped the Chairman's message to reach the hearts of the masses. Is it decadent, a skirt that barely covers the buttocks? Is it scandalous to see women as sex objects? "Don't be conservative!" That's what Party officials respond if you ask them about this 180-degree turnaround. The leopard has changed its spots. Or its skirt.

Sun Lin arrived in Beijing at exactly the same time as the first supermarket. The store, called Jialefu (Happy Family), belonging to the well-known French chain Carrefour, opened only a short distance from Sun Lin's employer's apartment. Right away the young peasant woman liked the place. It reminded her of a rural market with the various goods set up on one floor. The clients looked like normal Chinese people, dressed just about like she was—not like those nouveau-riche shoppers who buy fake perfume for 500 yuan a bottle. At Jialefu you fill your shopping cart with everyday products—just like a French consumer, happily, without thinking anything of it. There's only one problem: The customers don't have cars. Have you ever tried to get the contents of a shopping cart into a bike basket? Thank heaven for cheap taxis.

The store introduced a new kind of shopping in China. The first few days were madness, with shoppers leaving nothing in their wake, throwing everything into their carts, barely noticing what they were buying. Lack of respect for the speed limit led to shopping cart accidents. This kind of behavior shows the degree of frustration felt by people who have suddenly found that they could choose. There was violence in their gestures, and nervous joy. Professor Yao is right: Consumption is the only freedom Chinese people have—as long as they have the money to pay for it.

In the baked goods section, the crowd's enthusiasm almost led to a riot. There were ten or more employees wrapping cellophane around loaves of bread and buns, hot from the oven. Soon, in spite of their valiant efforts, the employees couldn't keep up with the pressing demands of the shoppers. In this tense situation—several shoppers were elbowing their neighbors quite brutally—one of the bakers had the idea to throw one, then two, then three loaves of bread up in the air, as if he were throwing food to animals at the zoo. This novel distribution method pleased the customers. They started to smile. The anxious waiting turned into a childish shoving match, with grown men and women leaping into the air to catch any loaf they could get their hands on. These mass-produced baked goods were supposed to give a taste of what French people eat for breakfast. The bakers of the Happy Family had their own idea of mass distribution. At least they prevented a riot.

People who have been ruled with an iron hand for forty years lose contact with the rules of conduct that are appropriate in the context of liberty and responsibility. The legendary patience of the Chinese people has been bitterly tried by the arrival of capitalism. As long as the stakes were low, there was no reason to think of one's neighbor as a dangerous rival. One had to figure out how to cope; people were resigned to "sharing the shortage." Abundance has transformed behavior, leading to impoliteness and violence. When they're waiting in a crowd, the Chinese push and shove—whether it is to buy a kilo of rice, to get into a movie theater, to mail a letter, or even to get on an airplane (although one is sure to get a seat). People seem incapable of controlling the rush of their desire. Fights break out on street corners for no reason. Belligerent motorists take revenge on one another, stopping on the ring road to fight over minor issues, blocking traffic for a quarter of an hour, to the great joy of the spectators who cry for more.

Every man for himself—that seems to be the new rule in the People's Republic of China. As for women and children, along with older people, they are the designated victims of male boorishness. A woman has to be pregnant, an elderly person tottering with illness, before a young man will give up his place on a crowded bus. The selfishness of some is complemented by the resignation of the others.

BON APPETIT

Like stores, luxury hotels and their shopping galleries have become popular spots for city people on the lookout for new experiences. Until 1990, these multi-star establishments were off limits to the local population, by order of the government, which, for political reasons, didn't want to see Chinese people mixing with foreigners, perhaps fearing that the Chinese might have the opportunity to taste forbidden fruit, decadent pleasures. Strangely, this edict harked back strangely to the sign found outside clubs and restaurants in 1930s Shanghai: CHINESE PEOPLE AND DOGS NOT ALLOWED. This prohibition was swept away by the Communists during "liberation." Fifty years later, history was repeating itself. The roles were reversed. Those same Communists were in the position of the rulers they had unseated.

As was the case in Shanghai, Chinese people accompanying foreigners could nonetheless enter the luxury hotels and thumb their noses at apartheid. Orders were that porters shouldn't bother clients. This policy could lead to comical exchanges in the lobbies of these establishments. Sometimes foreign businessmen would be approached by seductive young women who would simper, "May I come in with you?" Once inside, the couples immediately fell apart, to the surprise of the men, who doubtless chalked it up to the inscrutability of the Chinese.

It's ironic that what finally broke the prohibition against Chinese people entering luxury hotels was the Tiananmen Square massacres. The years 1989 and 1990 were dark times for international tourism and trade. Dozens of modern hotels had just been built to host the Asian Games in September 1990. Pragmatism finally prevailed over ideology: At a time when it was important to attract foreign currency into the country, it seemed ridiculous to refuse admission to four- and five-star hotels to Chinese people with their pockets bulging with dollars. The void created by the absence of foreign customers was rapidly filled by private entrepreneurs, nouveau-riche peasants, and civil servants with exorbitant expense accounts.

The buffet formula in hotel restaurants has had enormous success with Chinese diners who like to get good value for their money (even when it's not strictly *their* money). Mealtimes become balancing acts where, on one plate, rising high in the air with the greatest of ease—drum roll, suspense, there it is!—a pyramid of victuals. Three cheers! But wait. Is this an acrobatic show or a clown act? The little pieces of lemon on the smoked salmon are holding up a caramelized pastry, squeezed on the right by the duck à l'orange and on its left by the foie gras covered with a generous hill of white rice and buns. A thick dollop of chocolate mousse decorates the summit of this culinary mountain. It's a new kind of sweet-and-sour. And now for our next act… All this is hilarious to the Western observer. (For the Chinese, it's just as hilarious to see a "long nose" eating his spring roll with a fork after having started off his meal with soup—which, as any lover of Chinese cuisine knows, should be drunk at the end of the meal to help with digestion. So there.)

"There's no good meal without good wine." This saying has started to win followers among the nouveaux riches, who wash down their Western meals with red or white wine, saving the drinking of beer and traditional liquors for meals featuring Chinese food. In a country where beer dominates the market—800 breweries produce 1,500 varieties of beer—wine consumption is limited but growing. The snob appeal of wine and cognac could grow into widespread appreciation if the prices went down. Foreign wineries have started to lay the groundwork, setting up joint ventures and bottling various kinds of white, red, and rosé wines of acceptable price and quality. Think about it: What if every person in China drank only one liter of wine per month? Wine growers, like other foreign entrepreneurs, believe in the Chinese market.

With high standards and the appetite of an ogre, Professor Yao unfortunately cannot afford to treat himself to the kind of meal he would most enjoy. But he does often visit the palatial luxury hotels—not to admire the boutiques, nor to relax in the bar, but to go to the toilets.

The bathrooms at these hotels are as big as his apartment, equipped with stalls bigger than his kitchen, with shining tiles, impeccable lighting, paper softer than any Chinese person has in his home, sparkling sinks, and full-length mirrors. And they always smell fresh: "Even the shit smells luxurious here," says the professor, who is not ashamed of his somewhat scatological sense of humor. The epitome of luxury is the attention given the guest by the restroom attendant, often of an advanced age, dressed to the nines, as deferential as you could desire, who turns on the water faucet for you and gives you a towel for your hands, which may still be slightly damp despite your use of the electric hand dryer. The professor feels like a real pasha at such moments, which he drags out for as long as he can, getting assistance from start to finish (or just about). All of this happiness is free, free, free. In contrast, you have to pay for the socialist public toilets, which are dirty, stinking, and cold. "Who can still claim that socialism is superior to capitalism?" That's what Professor Yao said to his brother-in-law, teasing him, the day that he brought him in to show him perfection in the form of a toilet! A connoisseur, the professor has developed his own system to classify all of the best bathrooms in the capital. All of them are in hotels.

Public toilets are, indeed, in a sorry state. Like almost all public places in China, they are not respected by their users. You'd have to have quite an extraordinary commitment to the public good to take care of toilets equipped with one and only one drain. There are usually no dividing walls, or if there are, they're very low, and there's no door. The lack of comfort together with the deadly odor does not prevent some imperturbable users from reading their newspapers on the john, almost as if they were at home! For some, it's exactly as if they were at home; in old neighborhoods there are no toilets in the houses, and the street facilities are all there is. To resolve this public toilet crisis, which promotes the spread of diseases such as hepatitis and gives China a deplorable image in the sanitary department, the Beijing authorities have launched several contests for the best public toilet design. They have also organized expositions to encourage janitors and users to be more sensitive to matters of hygiene.

Professor Yao can't afford to eat in big hotels, so he settles for moderately priced restaurants. There are lots of them. The restaurant industry is one of the service industries that has grown the fastest since the economic system was loosened in 1992. There are restaurants for every budget, ranging from greasy spoons to luxury establishments and including Chinese and Western fast-food joints and night markets serving snacks. Every street in every village, town, or metropolis has its little group of restaurants. Often enough, there are too many of them, and fierce competition is raging. Each establishment is forced to adopt an aggressive commercial strategy, which can lead to results that are of dubious value aesthetically. For a while, the trend was statues of naked Greek and Roman goddesses in restaurant doorways. Unfortunately the presence of goddesses could not guarantee the quality of the food. Some restaurants close down almost as quickly as they open up; others, no matter what the caliber of their culinary offerings, prosper.

Food has always played a central role in Chinese culture. As purchasing power rises, more people eat out. Once a necessity, food becomes a pleasure. It's easy to find some dishes you like from among the amazing variety of Chinese cooking styles. Food is also the inescapable way to clinch a deal. Every contract is sealed with a drink or a meal. This is true all over the country, but certain regions are particularly well known—the province of Canton, for example. As the proverb says: "The Cantonese will eat anything that has legs, except tables and chairs!" In the south, as elsewhere, mass consumption has its downside. All too often, the restaurants try to serve as many customers as possible while the clients try to stuff themselves with the maximum amount of food in order to show that they have the money to do so. In the process the quality of the food suffers. But there is no food to throw away—rich or poor, the clients carry away the leftovers in their doggy bags.

At home as well, gustatory habits are evolving. Overall, people eat more and better. Only in the poorest regions do people eat just to survive. For some people, rampant inflation puts a damper on spending, but sacrifices are made in budgetary areas other than food. Children eat particularly well. Those little brown heads should get all they want to eat. Better still, they should never know the malnutrition their parents suffered. Down with the skinny, up with the chubby! Who cares about muscle tone, as long as there's plenty of fat! Doctors are getting worried about overeating, which presents serious dangers for the children. Obesity is a phenomenon that is starting to become apparent in the schoolyards. But parents don't want to hear about it. A round body has long been a symbol of wealth. As long as money is king, you'd better not show up all skin and bones like a beggar.

Professor Yao spends about half his earnings on food. When he's not going out to eat, he's eating well at home. In the West, he'd be called a bon vivant, someone who lives well, but this expression is still unknown in the Middle Kingdom, where so many have lived badly for so long. The professor's heart problems have forced him to cut down his consumption of his favorite foods, those richest in fat. He has also had to cut down on alcohol, limiting his beer drinking to only two liters per day instead of four. These are tough resolutions for him to keep. He gripes about his doctors: "Now that I have money, I'm supposed to restrain myself. I can hardly believe it."

In the past, students always limited themselves to the bad food that was available in campus cafeterias. Now, the professor has noticed, students treat themselves from time to time to a meal in a little restaurant or a drink in a bar in the university neighborhood. The standard of living is rising, he thinks as he bikes past café terraces full of cheerful young people clustered around glasses of Coke.

One day, when the summer heat had found its way into spring and the brutal heat of the sun forced cyclists to ride on the wrong side of the road in the shade of the plantain trees, the professor pulled his bike to a stop. For the first time in his fifty-seven years, he went into a café and quickly drank a cool beer, one from his daily quota. To heck with dieting! He paid 3 yuan to the smiling young waitress who radiated contagious good spirits, and sat for a moment contemplating the students at the next table. He remembered that in 1984, when his son and daughter were studying for their exams at the end of their university studies, he came home one evening with two big bottles of Coke to encourage them. One bottle each. What a party! He didn't tell his children how long he had hesitated before shelling out the money for the Cokes. They already knew he was just a poor teacher, no need to rub it in. These days, students don't need their parents to surprise them with their favorite drink. They go to coffee shops with their own pocket money.

FESTIVALS AND SUPERSTITIONS

As he got back on his bike, Professor Yao noticed how well the beer had quenched his thirst. The beer had been ice-cold. Economic liberalism has made refrigerators widespread. That's the end of warm beer. For that reason alone, Professor Yao prefers Deng to Mao. There's a more serious reason. He can never forgive the Great Helmsman for having massacred his students in 1989. They will never know the sweet pleasure of a carefree moment on the shady terrace of a café. This thought made him sad for a minute and he pedaled harder. He'd been pedaling for forty years.

He was in a hurry that day; he had to go to a wedding dinner. He would stuff himself without spending a single yuan. This idea cured him of the depression that had settled on his usually light spirits. Although the host of the wedding was of modest means, the food served at dinner would be abundant. It might well turn out to be excellent, too. Weddings are not occasions for skimping. You'd lose face. Weddings mean unbelievable banquets, in contrast with the simplicity of signing the marriage papers and doing without a religious ceremony. Marital union at the Civil Affairs Bureau is never more than a strict formality. The state representatives seem to be profoundly bored as they mechanically stamp marriage certificates one after the other on an old table of light varnished wood scattered with dusty newspapers and jars serving as tea cups. The mood would be more appropriate to a funeral than a wedding.

Because of the lack of ceremony, all the more emphasis is put on the wedding feast afterward. This is the life! Thousands, tens of thousands of yuan are squandered in a matter of hours by nouveau-riche hosts and also by proletarians who sometimes spend more than a year's salary on a wedding feast. Where do they get the money? It's hard to say. The issue becomes all the more mysterious when you consider that besides the wedding party, there's the groom's dowry. The dowry tradition is very much alive in rural areas, where the marriage price must be figured according to established guidelines. In the city, the word *dowry* has disappeared, but it's still the custom for a young man and his family to buy enough things to equip a household for the young couple. Considering the price of quality furniture and appliances these days—no one would dare buy cheap goods—this modern dowry adds up to several tens of thousands of yuan. There are a few more items on the bill. What about the bridal gown and the groom's suit? It is considered chic for Chinese city folk to get married in

Western clothes, even if this extravagance costs a fortune and violates the traditional association of white with death and funerals. Those who do not have the means to rent or buy a white gown and all the trappings can fake it by having their photo taken in a studio that provides the necessary accoutrements. There are photo services to fit every price range, from 500 to 5,000 yuan, depending on the type of gown and the competence of the studio, which can be deplorable. The custom of taking wedding photos in white arose in the 1980s in Shanghai, harking back to the earlier fashion of Shanghai aristocrats in the 1930s. Modern brides and grooms are proud to set their photo on the teak furniture in their living room.

Couples who are rich or aspiring to be rich don't trouble themselves with such strategies, which are the last resort of the penniless. They buy their outfits without looking at the price tags and push extravagance as far as it will go. It's a real hoopla. The bride and groom and the wedding party parade around in gleaming black limousines, rented for the occasion from taxi companies delighted with the windfall. The beautiful people in this caravan, which could be mistaken for an official procession if it weren't for the white ribbons stuck on the car doors, eventually meet up at a fancy restaurant.

Zhang Donghua has been to many of these grand weddings, and he always complains about the lack of spontaneity. Carefully held in check by their parents, who conscientiously supervise every activity, the bride and groom passively play out their roles as figureheads. As rigidly mapped out as music ledger paper, these banquets have the frigid atmosphere of political meetings. A master of ceremonies opens the evening by bellowing out in an official tone that would suit the General Secretary of the Communist Party: "Ladies and gentlemen, the marriage banquet has begun!" The guests then applaud mechanically, with the puppetlike gestures of members of the People's National Congress. One might also be reminded of a Party congress; the "Wedding March" replaces the "Internationale," but in either case the tune is already dictated.

The government still thinks it can dictate the behavior of the people in every area of their lives, and it has tried several times to wage war on the shocking "waste" of wedding feasts. Each time, the war has been lost. How can these reprimands be taken seriously? Newspapers controlled by the government call out in a moralizing tone for moderation, arguing that the country still counts millions of poor people, but on facing pages there are ads for fabulous products destined for the dream houses of young couples. Without repression, the old totalitarian reflexes lack effectiveness. It's hard to imagine the police charging into wedding banquets to arrest the participants.

Neighborhood committees and the Women's Association try to promote the Party line by organizing collective weddings. Ten or twenty couples celebrate their marriages together in a hall decorated with all the gay abandon of a church bake sale. There's an orchestra playing corny tunes, a speech by a Party official, and another one by one of the day's bridegrooms, chosen not for his talents as an orator but for his loyalty to the Party. Then there's a meal, one meal for everyone, a simple meal—a very simple meal that costs the collective very little and the couples almost nothing. Although collective weddings have been in existence for years, they have not gained widespread acceptance. Most couples detest the idea and refuse to play along, and even those who accept the ritual in order to avoid hassles also rush to organize their own private celebration for the next day. Of course, they invite the political officials of the neighborhood, who are only too happy to attend. Two weddings for the price of one! The Chinese just want to have fun, and they absolutely must show that they have the money to do so. No Party decree can change this.

Funerals also are becoming more and more expensive and sophisticated, featuring interminable processions, gigantic wreaths, videos, and professional mourners, all furnished by specialized companies offering a complete range of services à la carte. The funeral parlor business must be booming if the fad for fancy burials is any indication.

On this issue, a dispute whose outcome is uncertain pits the government, anxious to preserve the limited amount of arable land, against the people, who wish to bury their dead rather than incinerate them.

Burial is traditional. Despite official calls for cremating the dead, two-thirds of the deceased are laid to rest in the earth, where they occupy about 30,000 acres. Coffin production requires 2.3 million cubic yards of wood or the equivalent of the annual production of the Province of Fujian. In a country the size of China, the amount of space reserved for the dead may not seem outrageous. But the government points out that only 8 percent of Chinese land can be cultivated, and the population increases every year, adding 14 million new mouths to feed. Meanwhile, cereal production is declining, owing to natural catastrophes and the refusal of peasants to plant unprofitable crops such as wheat and corn. American analysts predict that China will lose 200 million tons of grain in the next century if the population continues to grow at the current rate and if the area of land under cultivation diminishes. The government wants at all costs to avoid wasting fertile land. Of course, the government itself has constructed many commercial buildings on good land.

In the rich coastal regions of the east such as Zhejiang, tombs are encroaching on the hills. Some peasants do not hesitate to construct vaults on plots of arable land, in the hopes of facilitating the voyage of their dear one to the other world. The authorities are fighting back: In Ningbo, a large provincial port, they more or less ordered the inhabitants to incinerate their dead as of October 1, 1996. At that time, cremations constituted only 17 percent of the funerals in the city. In Shanghai, where 13 million souls live crowded together but where people have money to spend, the number of funeral lots sold per year is more than 50,000, and all told burial sites occupy an area of about 100,000 square meters. The municipal authorities estimate that if they built six-story buildings on this land it would be possible to house 10,000 families in new three-room apartments. Worried about this state of affairs, the officials of China's most populous city have proposed new solutions, such as burials in walls or, more ecologically, in trees, without much success. Out of 100,000 who died in Shanghai in 1995, only 4,691 were walled up and 54 were placed in trees.

Well-to-do Beijing citizens can end up buried near the four emperors of the Qing dynasty, the last and most famous emperor, Pu Yi, who is buried in a cemetery situated 93 miles to the east of the capital, opened in 1995. How chic. A simple plot costs 2,500 yuan, plus 500 yuan to cover the fee that would have been paid for cremation. A tomb in sculpted marble is worth more than 50,000 yuan. On the one hand, the government encourages cremation, and on the other, it gives the green light to schemes like this. Trapped in the liberal economic logic, the authorities seem powerless to combat tradition and superstition.

To return to weddings: the choice of dates follows the rules of geomancy, a "science" that is making a comeback in China. A wedding that takes place in an even month on an even day means double happiness. More sophisticated rules favor the eighth and the eighteenth of May, dates that are pronounced in the Cantonese dialect as "I am getting rich" and "I am going to get rich." These two dates are booked months in advance at restaurants and taxi companies. The eighteenth is the most sought after because, besides symbolizing wealth, it is a propitious date to pay tribute to one's ancestors—and to set oneself up in business. This is according to a three-thousand-year-old almanac of Chinese astrology that is well known in Taiwan and Hong Kong and once again popular on the mainland after having been banned. Superstitions are so fashionable that families try to plan the date of birth for their children for the eighth, the eighteenth, or the twenty-eighth, anything as long as it contains the number *8*, which means "get rich" in Cantonese. Soon they'll be planning the date for deaths as well.

Some fans of almanacs use them—or misuse them—in a more mundane fashion. If astrologers proclaim that it's better not to go out on such and such a day, these believers call in sick to work! What a good excuse for goldbrickers, the official press complains, never missing an occasion to denounce superstition. It's no good. How many campaigns against superstition has the Chinese Communist Party waged since 1949? Ten? Twenty? To no avail. The tendency is irreversible: the Chinese will do whatever they want. But that doesn't mean they can say whatever they want. They can only whisper.

YOUNG PEOPLE BREAK LOOSE

The declaration of individual liberty and the scorn for official recommendations are very pronounced among the young, who are influenced by Western trends and lifestyles. The discothèque, absent from the Chinese scene in the 1980s, constitutes one of the symbols of this liberty in the 1990s. Big cities have dozens, often set up within a few months of each other and competing with each other in size (grandeur always impresses the Chinese) and ultramodern technology; they're every bit as impressive as European or American clubs. Perched on bars set in the middle of the dance floors, hostesses warm up the room. They're usually wearing a strict minimum to excite the dancers who, as the evening wears on, shed their inhibitions.

For many young Chinese people, dancing is a way to discover that they have bodies, that their bodies are their own. One does not have to be a rigid automaton whose body has been shaped by obligatory exercises in recreation classes, with movements carried out to the rhythm of a military march or molded by sports schools as an instrument for Communist and nationalist propaganda; the body can be more than a sad incarnation of collectivist rape.

The first steps taken on the dance floor are awkward, the torso is stiff, the arms are in the way, the eyes are anxiously watching the others. But what a contrast, what a change in only a few years. What a victory over revolutionary frustration. What happiness for young Chinese people to move freely, simply, without being judged, graded, put on record, indoctrinated! It's an immeasurable joy that cleanses the spirit.

While one might hesitate to assert that discothèques with their repetitive music arouse the human intellect, they surely have a salutary effect on the human body, especially for individuals who have been forced to keep in line, to sacrifice their own development in the name of the supreme interests of the country. In the discothèque, young people learn that they can be masters of their bodies, if they so desire, in freedom. They're going wild.

Their abandon is worrisome to the establishment. The *People's Daily* clamors for "healthy" leisure activities—which discothèques most definitely are not. The definition of "healthy" leisure activities in the (little) dictionary of the Chinese Communist Party is any activity that won't give young people nasty ideas. The definition of a nasty idea is an idea that the Communist Party doesn't like. The Party doesn't like much. But the market economy has a way of imposing its own rules.

The spectacular takeoff of the discothèque was soon surpassed by that of the karaoke, now at the height of popularity. With this Japanese invention, a person sings into a microphone to accompanying music while the words scroll past on a video screen. It's a runaway hit in China. If you've ever dreamt of becoming a variety star, karaoke gives you the three-minute illusion that you've found your true calling. While you sing along to a saccharine little song, you can parade around in front of an equally cloying background of beach scenes and couples, just like the real stars. There's warm applause for any one-night crooner who sings approximately in tune. Spectators had better be understanding; they may find themselves on the other side of the spotlights later in the evening.

"OK." That's what it says in bright lights outside these establishments. These omnipresent signs are to be found in every town in China: either "OK" or "KTV," for Karaoke Television. Karaoke has become an institution for a people who love to sing—and not just "Mao is our sun" and "Without the Communist Party, there will be no new China." The equipment ranges from a simple TV and VCR with a karaoke function that are placed together on the wobbly Formica table at a village hangout, all the way to the ultramodern equipment of the entertainment palaces where playing your song can cost 100 yuan, and including the festival halls of state businesses, which invariably have the necessary setup. It's not uncommon to see hospitals that are lacking in basic materials but are equipped with a beautiful karaoke set.

The biggest karaokes have private salons that are luxuriously furnished and well supplied with music and video materials and female staff. The young women are modestly called hostesses. Zhang Donghua knows several good addresses for the nouveaux riches, where the TVs project images that are not quite so sickly sweet, and the hostesses' role is not limited to serving drinks and songs.

Since the Chinese love to eat and love to sing, they love "RTV." The R stands for "restaurant." You eat, you sing—and you drink, which helps a lot. Of course, you shouldn't sing with your mouth full, though some do. Every banquet hall has its own equipment, which differs according to the caliber of the establishment. A major restaurant without karaoke is heading straight for bankruptcy.

There is a lot of money to be made from this craze for karaoke and discothèques. Some owners, in their rush for quick profits, disregard basic safety rules. Witness the following dramatic events. On November 27, 1994, there were 234 deaths in a fire at a nightclub in Fuxin, in the province of Liaoning. In December 1994 there were 324 deaths, most of them children, in a fire in a cinema in Kamaray in Xinjiang. In April 1995 there were 51 deaths in a fire at a karaoke in Urumuqi, also in Xinjiang. These are only the worst disasters. In China, accidents involving fewer than ten deaths are rarely reported by the media.

Two boards, three pieces of sheet metal, a scrap of carpeting, a neon sign, and you're in business. There are no building codes and licensing regulations. The places are built with the simplest materials, and it's just too bad if they're flammable. Too bad if there is no emergency exit, no fire extinguisher, or other minor details—as long as everything looks flashy enough to dazzle an ignorant clientele thirsty for fun. What about the authorities, the safety officials, the police? They close their eyes to these violations, as the press hastens to point out once a catastrophe has already happened. The authorities can be propitiated with free evenings, banknotes, and lady companions— and these same authorities are responsible for fighting social plagues like corruption and prostitution.

How else do the Chinese people spend their free time? Playing games—cards, billiards, Chinese checkers, and, of course, mah-jongg, the national game. They play a lot, and for a lot of money. Gambling's forbidden? Not if you stay behind closed doors! Mah-jongg, a form of dominos, was forbidden during the Cultural Revolution—although, as was the case with dancing, Western films, and luxury products, the prophets of asceticism were exempted from such prohibitions. They wallowed in gambling and pretty girls while the people were learning the Little Red Book by heart, afraid of being tortured and imprisoned if they forgot an essential passage. Since then, the clack of dominos on kitchen tables during the long night hours, mixed with the merry clinking of glasses and bottles of beer and liquor, hasn't bothered any-one. Betting is tolerated as long as it's done in private.

DISRESPECT FOR THE ENVIRONMENT

Today millions of people in China are engaged in debauchery and stag-gering consumption and could care less about the public good, which brings up a crucial question for the country's future: Who's taking out the garbage? What about the mountains of waste that surround cities and litter the countryside? Take the case of the two "earthly paradises," Hangzhou and Suzhou, not far from Shanghai. These two cities are among those most visited by Chinese tourists, the first for its West Lake and hill of tea, the other for its gardens and canals. Suzhou was known by the pompous nickname "Venice of the Orient" even before pollution started to tarnish the city. The canals of Suzhou give off a stench that would make the city of the doges seem delicately perfumed. People and businesses use the water as a dump, seemingly ignorant of the fact that they are killing the goose that lays the golden eggs.

Realizing too late the breadth of the disaster, the municipality took steps to clean up the canals and rehabilitate part of the natural habitat that had fallen into ruins. They even called in the famous Chinese-American architect I. M. Pei to redesign the city of his ancestors so that water and gardens would once again unite in a majestic combination and lend nobility to this vacation spot that was dear to Marco Polo and is one of the oldest cities in the Yangtze Valley.

As for Hangzhou, a site that inspired the great poets of the Tang dynasty, the lake there is clean and its shores relatively so, but the hills around are littered with piles of refuse—waste paper, Coke cans, plastic bottles, used Kleenex, and all the household garbage you could ask for. Near the Baoshan pagoda, the rocky heights overlooking the lake have become garbage dumps. Curiously, crowds of young lovers still congregate there; couples will sit or lie among items of garbage that are either encrusted, fossil-like, in the surface of the earth, or blowing about in the breeze. The revolting odor doesn't seem to dampen the allure of romance, even in the summer season, when the heat kicks in. Across the way, on the south bank of the lake, the cool magnificent hill of the Jade Emperor is not faring any better. The path leading to the Taoist temple is flanked on each side by long furrows of trash, testimony to excessive consumption and a total disrespect for the environment.

Older Chinese people, for decades obliged to tighten their belts, had no reason to be sensitive to environmental questions. (This was on the individual level; industrial pollution was already wreaking havoc.) Young consumers are not any more concerned than their elders. The question of the environment is not brought up in school or at home—or very seldom. Whether they are walking through the streets of their city, or driving down a country road, or going on an excursion on the Yellow River, the Chinese don't burden themselves with their garbage. Kids throw everything on the ground. Their parents don't say a word; they do the same themselves. It's as if there were no tomorrow. Maybe they tell themselves that out of 1.2 billion people, there's got to be someone to pick up the garbage. But it's not manpower that's lacking; it's willpower—and policies. As it slowly comes to terms with the dangers of pollution, the government timidly attacks those who damage the environment. But an ounce of prevention and a cupful of repression don't guarantee improvement. What about education? That is where the problem lies: for millions of consumers, the protection of the environment is the least of their worries. Experts estimate that there will be an increase in garbage of at least 10 percent per year until the year 2005: China produced 100 million tons of waste in 1995, twice that produced in 1985. The situation is urgent.

Pollution in China is not only a result of the negligence of individuals. Industries contribute greatly to the degradation of the land, water, and air. According to the National Agency for the Protection of the Environment, at the end of 1993 about one third of the total surface of the country was affected by acid rain caused essentially by sulfur dioxide emissions from burning coal, the primary means of generating energy in China. "Make the polluters pay" is the new watchword. A pilot project produced a 30 percent decline in the pollution level in regions where businesses had to pay a tax according to waste they produced. The hunt is on for factories that pollute rivers and lakes, where the damage is increasing considerably. The case of the Huaihe River was particularly serious. This river crosses big agricultural regions in the east and is the source of drinking water for 1.5 million people. It is also one of the most polluted rivers in the country: 1.6 billion cubic yards of untreated waste are dumped into its waters every year. Fortunately, the government reacted to the disastrous situation and managed to get help from the World Bank.

The national budget for fighting pollution was 25 billion yuan for the period 1996-2000. This is only 0.8 percent of the gross national product. The future of China's environment will depend on the will of local authorities to attack the problem. But they have so many other problems that it is difficult for them to make saving the environment a priority—especially at a time when productivity is the dogma.

Officials in big cities deal with the most visible ecological problems by cleaning up the downtown areas. This is quite an achievement, considering the dimensions of Chinese cities. This urban cleanliness always surprises foreign visitors, who rarely stray from the beaten path. Outside of the tourist circuits, the grim reality reveals itself. Barely constructed, the new quarters crumble under the filth, strewn with heaps of household trash wafted by the wind. Waste paper and plastic bags cling to trees and bushes, side by side with kites swept from the hands of children.

Chapter Five

A CHANGE OF SCENE

When the Wang family finally stepped across the threshold of their new apartment, they had been waiting for a long time.

Two years earlier, they had been evicted from their two-room apartment in Yonganli quarter. The entire quarter (to the east of the capital, in the business and embassies district of Chaoyang) was to be destroyed, to make room for imposing high-rises, full of offices to be rented or sold at astronomical rates. Hundreds of families had been thrown out onto the street.

But then the rumor had been circulating for months: They're going to raze the quarter. But the future always seems far away. No one's bags were packed when the nasty notices appeared announcing the imminent arrival of the bulldozers. The tenants were summoned before the neighborhood housing office. They were told that they would be compensated, that they would have provisional housing while they waited, supposedly for one year, for new apartments in another neighborhood.

This announcement fell like a bomb on the inhabitants of this block of gray brick buildings, built with the help of the Russians in the 1950s during a period of Sino-Soviet friendship. The municipality, the owner of the site, had managed the buildings in a low-key and typically socialist fashion, charging minimal rents and providing no upkeep. At the end of 1993, at the time of the expulsions, the rents were a symbolic 10 yuan per month. The municipality was losing money and claimed that the cost of electricity, gas, and water alone exceeded the rent collected. A long overdue renovation would cost more than demolition and reconstruction. No, the municipality had another plan—a juicier one. The real estate company's vision did not seem to be much different from what was going on in other Chinese cities and in many parts of the capitalist world: an anarchic process of urban renewal featuring building a business center and forcing the local residents to the outskirts of the city. That, too, is socialism with Chinese characteristics.

The tenants of Yonganli were only too aware that conditions in their quarter were unsanitary. They wanted more comfortable apartments, and they were ready to pay a bit more to get them. But why move all the way across town? And why right away before the first stone of their new apartment buildings had been laid? Furthermore, they were asked to pay a down payment on their future apartments when the site hadn't even been chosen. "To have to advance 100 yuan per square meter for an apartment that hasn't even been built, and who knows when it will be??! It's scandalous. We know all about their promises," protested one tenant.

The "provisional" housing provided was about 9 miles away, in barracks without running water or heat and far from any form of public transportation. "In the name of the Communist ideal, they forced people to live in mediocre conditions for forty years, and now, in the name of the market economy, they send them out to the suburbs without giving them any choice," an old man shouted at the officials in the housing office. "Do you think we're idiots?" The anxiety of the inhabitants was based on their awareness of similar cases where expelled tenants waited for their new housing for more than four years instead of the promised year.

The Yonganli evictions led to resistance. The tenants declared war.

Of course, there was little hope of their winning such an unequal combat. But the tenants still thought they might limit the damage by delaying the expulsions long enough to get organized to fight for lowering the amount of the down payment and to insist on decent provisional housing.

The tenants' resolve was strengthened when they found out that the son of Chen Xitong, a powerful Party official in Beijing, was a key player in the project. Chen Junior was one of the directors of a real estate company that was part of a joint venture involving some Japanese investors. The people of Beijing have a ferocious hatred for Chen Xitong, the Party Committee Secretary, who, besides being notoriously corrupt, was one of those responsible for the repression in 1989.

On the evening of June 3 of that infamous year, the people of Yonganli had seen the tanks and trucks rolling by their windows on the way to Tiananmen Square to carry out the biggest massacre in the history of the People's Republic of China. For the first time since the Tangshan earthquake in 1976, the ground beneath Beijing was trembling—under the infernal treads of the tanks. Some people threw stones at the mammoth, terrifying vehicles. In vain. The more courageous tried to stop the tanks at Dabeiyao crossroads, a bit farther to the north, by building flaming barricades. There were many dead and wounded. In the ensuing days, the army coldheartedly hunted down the last few insurgents who were still hiding out in the neighborhood, unable or unwilling to flee. Demonstrators were finished off in the stairwells. These terrible images are engraved on the collective memory of the people and can never be erased.

The tenants at Yonganli knew that they couldn't keep the municipality from demolishing their buildings. But they were not ready to be thrown out on the street like dirt by Chen Xitong the executioner. When you've defied tanks, should you fear bulldozers? Intelligent and sarcastic, the people of Yonganli considered theirs a struggle for human rights. They were taking literally the government slogan that human rights in China are not the same as in the West, that these rights concern first of all housing, food, and education. The tenants knew that the Communist regime pointed to the legions of homeless in the West as a rejoinder when the democracies took them to task about human rights. The Yonganli protesters also wanted to denounce real estate wheeling and dealing involving municipal bigwigs. Other neighborhoods had already rebelled against the local government's complicity in this brand of "urban planning," where, in the name of building a modern city adapted to the needs of the market economy, the local authorities turned a blind eye to every possible abuse. Real estate scandals attract notice in other cities besides Beijing, and demonstrations have broken out here and there, but in terms of real estate speculation, Beijing is the champion.

One scandal that caused quite a stir in the highest circles was the "Orient Plaza" affair. In planning the construction of this shopping center in the heart of Beijing, right next to the Forbidden City, the municipality blithely violated all the architectural norms and, it was rumored, accepted bribes from the Hong Kong company that was in charge of the project. The construction of the project was overseen by Hong Kong millionaire Li Kashing, who is a fervent supporter of the Communist regime, but the project had never received the go-ahead from the central authorities. The construction of this shopping center was finally halted against a backdrop of political rivalries at the top.

Certain deputies of the National People's Congress and some respected architects opposed to the initial project took advantage of the political conflict and sent a petition to the government calling for the plans to be revised. This action indirectly allowed protesters to criticize the suspect conditions under which the project had first been undertaken. After waiting in limbo for more than a year, construction began again once the project was modified and the changes approved at the top levels.

At the same time that the Yonganli mobilization was occurring, another housing protest movement was stirring to the west of the capital in the Xidan sector where many dignitaries of the regime lived, including the patriarch Deng Xiaoping. In the early morning of November 20, 1995, a hundred Beijing demonstrators, including retired people, suddenly materialized as if out of nowhere and sat down in front of the main entrance of the residence of Zhongnanhai (the Central and Southern Sea), headquarters of the Communist Party and home to several high dignitaries. What a surprise for the protectors of this building that is so symbolic of the regime!

The demonstrators were protesting efforts to expel them from their homes, traditional houses with square courtyards. Some were homeowners who objected to the sums offered for their property by the real estate executive, part of a state real estate company. Vacant lots in the neighborhood were being sold for 40,000 yuan per square meter to Sino-Asian joint venture companies, but the state real estate executive was offering the homeowners compensation of 800 yuan per square meter. According to the authorities, the state would use the money made from reselling the lots to build quality housing for the people who were being evicted, but the proposed new apartments were the usual substitute housing, mediocre and remote.

The historic Zhongnanhai protest—there hadn't been one since May 1989— denounced the collusion of the real estate company with the municipality, the police, and the justice system. The ties among these organizations were indeed so tight that the demonstrators were promptly carted off and locked up for an entire day in the offices of the real estate executive, where they were guarded by the police. "At first we refused to get into the buses under police pressure, and then, to avoid any incidents that might endanger the elderly, we gave in because they told us we could talk with the sector authorities," one of the demonstrators told the press. A national daily, one local TV station, and a foreign correspondent collected accounts. The Chinese journalists were not given permission to print the story. "They lied to us and locked us up illegally," one man said. He decided to go to court, and others followed suit. This muscle-flexing operation, intended to intimidate the demonstrators and quiet their claims, only increased their anger. The local court was deluged with complaints about illegal expulsion. The situation was absurd: One of the vice presidents of the court was himself moonlighting for 3,000 yuan per month giving legal advice to a real estate company.

Yao Hong, the daughter of Professor Yao, was on the front lines of the Yonganli combat, urging the tenants to stand firm and the authorities to compromise. With a small group of diehards, she organized a demonstration that rallied a hundred people in front of the office of Chen Xitong in the old neighborhood of the foreign missions. In the middle of the night, an elderly woman demonstrator fainted, and only then did a secretary of the mandarin finally deign to receive a delegation. The local press never reported the incident, but nonetheless news spread rapidly throughout the sector by word of mouth ("Chinese telephone").

EIGHT SQUARE METERS BY THE YEAR 2000

Yao Hong, thirty-two, had been living in Yonganli with her husband Wang Tong and their daughter, Ning Ning, for five years. She had taken over the apartment of her parents when they managed to move closer to the universities where they taught. The apartment consisted of two rooms of 10 and 8 square meters, badly lit by tiny windows, one kitchen, and a bathroom shared with three other families. With 6 or 7 square meters per person, the family's living space was close to the national norm. Before they moved to Yanganli, they had been living in a real dump, a studio apartment that had become extremely cramped once the baby was born.

To resolve the housing shortage, the government has made a commitment to build 150 million square meters per year, as compared with 33 million in 1994. This is part of the ninth five-year plan

(1996-2000), in part financed by private capital. The goal: to raise the average living area to 8 square meters per person by the end of the century.

The authorities are also encouraging people to think about becoming owners, a notion that has not yet seduced the Chinese, with the exception of the minority that are attracted by investments and speculation. The gradual phasing out of socialist housing with its symbolic rents may well change the Chinese attitude toward home ownership—that is, if property costs fall. Owning real estate is still too expensive for the average Chinese person who can pay rent of 30 to 50 yuan without difficulty.

After the Yonganli protest, the housing office tried to placate Yao Hong by offering her an apartment that was bigger than she had a right to. Unlike other protest leaders who were bought off, Hong refused to make such a pact with the devil. She also refused to go live in the municipality's barracks. Through friends, she and her family managed to sublet a moderately priced studio apartment. The housing office finally agreed to pay a small compensation to the residents who had been evicted and to reduce the down payment required for their future apartment. The protest thus achieved something on a practical level. Furthermore, the movement showed the people's capacity to mobilize on issues touching daily life; it sent a warning to the government that corruption should not determine what happens in housing. In fact, according to studies that have appeared in the Chinese press, these two issues—corruption and housing—are the principal preoccupations of citizens, who accord them greater importance than education and social security.

Two years after they left their home at Yonganli (not one year later as promised), the Wang family finally opened the door of their brand-new apartment. At last, they had their own bathroom and kitchen. No more lining up with neighbors to wash, go to the bathroom, or cook; no more forced chatter about everything and nothing. No more crowding. Professor's Yao's daughter and her husband had been waiting ten years for this moment. Her father made fun of her, saying, "Stop feeling sorry for yourself. I had to wait thirty years before I could relieve myself in peace in my own home!"

To have the key to a brand-new apartment does not necessarily mean that you can move in that evening—or the next day—or the day after that. That would be too simple. This is China, remember? A new apartment is just four walls, a floor, and a ceiling. Everything has to be finished and fixed up. It generally costs a tenant from 10,000 to 30,000 yuan, depending on the material used, to finish a 35 square meter apartment like that of the Wang family. Many people just don't have that kind of money. For those who do, their troubles are far from over. They have to find competent workmen and quality materials. With all of the emigrants ready to accept any job, there's no problem finding willing labor; but good intentions don't make someone a painter, a tile layer, or a plumber. The businesses that hire these pseudo-craftsmen tend to push for speedy, slapdash work so that they can move on and make more money elsewhere.

Many Chinese entrepreneurs, public and private, seem not to have grasped the idea that professionalism leads to consumer loyalty and long-term success. Or perhaps they simply know and don't care, knowing that the economic boom means that demand is greater than supply and will continue to be so for many more years—during which time they will be able to save enough money to invest elsewhere. The consumer pays the price for this shortsightedness. One month after the workmen leave, the paint cracks, the faucets leak, and the tiles gap, while the doorbell moans painfully and the lock on the front door obstinately refuses to turn.

But it's *cha bu duo*—"close enough." For decades everything has been *cha bu duo* in China. The phrase is used twenty times a day. Resigned, the Chinese have got used to these approximations in daily life. Now they're the ones paying for *cha bu duo*; it's no longer the government's job. Furious, they console themselves that their housing conditions are improving with time. Let's get that apartment fixed up.

Death to cockroaches! Unfortunately, these good intentions do not extend to the care of the shared parts of buildings, which look as if they were twenty years old after six months. No one keeps up the stair-wells or worries that the garbage is collected once in a blue moon. If the tenants were more united and responsible, the common areas would look quite different. But don't ask the Chinese to take charge of their neighborhood. They just got rid of totalitarian collectivism. "The responsibility of each person ends at his or her door sill," says Yao Hong. She herself does no more than her neighbors to improve the conditions outside her apartment.

On the other hand, she and her husband spare no pains in clean-ing their little nest, which is soiled by the grime of nearby construction sites. The dust invades the farthest reaches of the apartment, insidi-ously inserting itself behind the furniture that they so enjoyed buying at the Da Chao store. The name of this store makes them laugh because if you change the pronunciation, it means "orgasm." Wang Tong used to make his wife blush by suggesting that they go to Da Chao to choose a bed!

After 1992, big furniture stores opened up in the city. Prior to that, the Chinese made do with a few wholesale warehouses, all of which sold the same goods. Today stores go so far as to offer services that seem surprising in Communist China—things like delivery, assembly, and even reimbursement for the unsatisfied customer. What a miracle! Equally miraculous: By the year 2000 almost all urban households will be connected to a telephone network. Of course, the price of installing a telephone remains prohibitive: It had risen to 5,000 yuan by the end of 1996. The Chinese may have to break their piggy banks, but they'll get a phone. It's a matter of face. The richest already have portables to play with, and they blithely chat away in public.

The overview of Chinese interior decoration would be incom-plete without the centerpiece: the television. In the city it's color, in the countryside, black-and-white. Professor Yao's children remember that their family was one of the first in their building to have a black-and-white television. The neighbors used to bring their benches in the evening to watch the magic box. The professor had decorated the TV with an imitation color test pattern made out of paper, which he took off before each viewing and carefully taped back on afterward. In spite of the gradual increase in living space per person, the size of apartments remains modest, but the size of TVs is growing and growing. Whether on or off, a TV set is there to be seen. The same is true of sofas, whose dimensions are generally not well adapted to the puny apartments. Go and try to find a small sofa in a store! It's impossible. Furthermore, they're sold with two matching armchairs. In the middle of the living room reigns, then, the TV set, preferably Japanese. What do the Chinese do when they don't go out? Watch TV? No, they devour it.

BREAKING THE SILENCE OF SOCIALISM

Television has changed a lot in China. The broadcast area is much broader, and every village has at least one antenna. There are at least two thousand local, regional, and national channels, as well as cable. The content of the programming is becoming more varied. The big national channels still serve up the same old reheated propaganda, but regional TV aims to amuse, offering foreign films and sports. But all television programs are produced under the watchful eye of the Party, whose frequent "cleanup" operations culminate in temporary or permanent shutdowns of stations that are discovered to be transmitting or distributing programs considered politically incorrect or pornographic. Authorities in certain cities allow quite a bit of latitude. The government is hard put to control the development of the entertainment industry, which is caught up in the devilish, frenzied spiral of a market economy. Authorities in small cities—Party members who are expected to apply central directives to the letter—are nonetheless influenced by the commercial notion of viewer satisfaction. A show that wins the approval of the TV audience earns important advertising revenues, and these go into local coffers. Cable subscribers (who numbered 30 million at the end of 1994, and whose numbers are expected to double by the year 2000) also prefer entertainment to the ponderous shows broadcast over national TV. A cable subscription is only 1 yuan a month, but a yuan is a yuan, even for the well-to-do. City authorities know all this and close their eyes to films with questionable content.

Foreign producers wishing to sell programs to local channels find it impossible to negotiate freely. The major production companies, most of them American, are clamoring for the opening of the Chinese market, a market that certain producers, perhaps overly hastily, called "the most promising of the twenty-first century." They'll have to be patient, because it'll take a while to conquer this market.

One shouldn't expect to see political debates or films that are critical of the political regime on Chinese TV screens, whether in Beijing or 2,000 miles away. Censorship is still tight. But some things do slip through the cracks. At the beginning of 1996, a landmark series was aired on Beijing TV, and a good forty other channels picked it up. *Liu, the Hunchback Prime Minister*, broke records in terms of its viewing audience. The show took on the taboo subject of corruption in high places. True, the plot was set in the nineteenth-century Qing dynasty, but the corruption, power struggles, and conspiracies among top state officials evoked for Chinese viewers the period at the end of Deng Xiaoping's reign when the Communist regime, rotten to the core, was prey to frenetic internal struggles over succession. A masterpiece of intentional or unintentional parody, the series sold like hot cakes. Ad revenues doubled during the time that the forty daily episodes aired.

In China the TV is always on, hooked up to the VCR, playing pirated videos. The hi-fi is blaring. The telephone is ringing—after all, calls don't cost much. The high decibel level in big apartment buildings goes on into the wee hours, because the Chinese like late nights. It's a new mood, a big change from the former calm of socialist countries where the only nightlife consisted of spying on your neighbor, as quietly as possible.

There's another new noise: animal sounds. Actually, the bird sounds—squawking and tweeting—aren't new; pet birds have been part of homelife in China for centuries, and in parks at dawn you can see the birds with their elderly owners whose passion remains wholehearted. It's the meowing and barking that are new phenomena. To walk a dog or play with a cat is no longer a reprehensible manifestation of a "bourgeois character." High Party leaders, nonetheless, hesitate to be seen in public with their favorite pooch, in case the policy should suddenly change. Goldfish, birds, and cats are all right, but the strict regulation of dogs suggests a possible return to prohibition.

When restrictions were loosened, the fad for keeping pet dogs took the government by surprise. (The government seems to be continually surprised by the desires of the people it supposedly represents.) In the stampede to find a dog, some ignorant or credulous buyers have purchased unvaccinated animals or animals carrying disease. Rural people, the main suppliers of dogs, make a juicy profit on the market—and the profit is all the juicier if the seller doesn't have to pay veterinary fees. Some peasants have made the dog business their main occupation, traveling hundreds of miles to sell their animals in big cities—without bothering to make sure that the dogs aren't rabid.

After several years of dog frenzy, the government, claiming that the abundance of dogs endangered public health and hygiene, established a more rigorous policy. Only little dogs were to be allowed in the city, and the pets had to be registered with the local authorities. The fee for a Beijing dog license varies from 3,000 to 5,000 yuan, depending on the breed—a hefty sum. County authorities ask for more than 10,000 yuan, so legal dog ownership is out of reach for all but the very rich. (These regulations apply only in the city; in the countryside, dogs romp around in freedom, unlicensed. In any case, the peasants would never be able to pay these fees.) The new rulings are supposedly geared to reducing the number of bites and deaths from rabies.

It's easy to mask one's prejudices by invoking the need for hygiene and health. Revolutionary taboos die hard. Many leaders still argue that it's indecent to maintain an expensive hound in a country where not everyone has enough to eat—a specious argument that is also heard in richer countries.

Big dogs are thus uncommon sights in Chinese streets. An unlicensed dog may be put to sleep. The police carry out extermination campaigns against "man's best friend," and the results are published in the press as in the good old Maoist days, along with the results of campaigns against pests, sparrows, and insects that are ruining crops. Today dog owners who don't register their dogs face a fine as high as 20,000 yuan, and there's a prison term for repeat offenders. In Beijing, dog catching and the imposition of the assessing of a licensing fee have reduced the number of dogs by 110,000 between May 1995 and May 1996. The restaurants should have ample opportunity to stock up.

The slaughter of dogs may seem intolerable to Westerners, but Chinese people do tend to see dogs as dinner. Dogmeat is highly valued and can be found occasionally on restaurant menus or in special restaurants. The Chinese, especially in the south, have a reputation for eating the strangest things, including monkeys and serpents—why not dogs and cats? In the markets of Canton Province, perfumed by one thousand spices, chickens, rabbits, and cats sit side by side in cages, waiting to be boiled in huge smoking metal vats and then carved up, sold, and eaten. That's just the way it is. When it comes to animals, the Chinese tend to be less softhearted than Westerners. After Beijing's failed bid to host the Olympic Games in the year 2000, a rumor circulated in the capital: Disappointed and furious that their rival, Sydney, had won the bid, the Chinese were throwing stones at kangaroos in the zoo! It's just a tale, but no one was shocked; they found the idea funny.

When they're not out catching dogs, the police have other business: chasing criminals and delinquents.

CRIME AND PUNISHMENT

Until well into the 1980s, the Chinese lived in an environment that was practically free of violence (except state violence). Now the crime rate is climbing in a worrisome manner. The context of this trend is the rising standard of living and rapid urbanization. By the year 2000, the urban population should reach 450 million souls, concentrated mainly in a thousand sprawling metropolises. This figure does not take into account the populations in towns and "small" cities, each of which may have more than 100,000 people. There'll be a lot of work for the building industry—and a lot of work for criminals, especially if wealth continues to be so unequally distributed. Big cities in China remain among the safest in the world, but the atmosphere is steadily deteriorating. Recently established police patrols, drowning in the masses of people on the street, can't turn back the tide.

Attesting to the decline in urban life are the numerous citizens who report being mugged, robbed, or raped. The Chinese press provides abundant details. Petty crimes are exploited for their propaganda value—not in an effort to analyze deeper causes, but to justify repression. Official figures indicate an upsurge in criminality; in the absence of entirely reliable statistics, one can get an idea of the magnitude of the problem by looking at the number of prison sentences and executions reported in the papers and at the number of anticrime campaigns. The worst year since the launching of economic reforms was 1983, when 10,000 people were executed in the second half of the year. A bullet in the neck; that's how it's done. This "cleanup" of crime hasn't had the intended deterrent effect. Criminality and delinquency have spread, particularly among people under the age of twenty-five.

In the spring of 1996, the government launched a national "strike hard" campaign against crime, which led to an impressive number of arrests, convictions, and executions. A partial count indicated that more than 2,000 had died by the end of 1996, when the government announced an "open-ended prolongation of the operation."

During the first few months of the campaign, the press daily trumpeted its "great successes": drug operations dismantled, arms traffickers annihilated, armed robberies solved in the twinkling of an eye. This instantaneous and miraculously bountiful harvest made international human rights organizations suspicious. How could so many tens of thousands of criminals have been arrested, tried, sentenced, and in some cases executed, so quickly? Police the world over should come take lessons from the Chinese! The official order to "strike hard" unleashed operations on a scale unprecedented prior to 1983. Two possible explanations can be advanced for this "success": Either the degree of criminality is such that the police had only to reach out and scoop up the troublemakers; or, in normal circumstances, the forces of law and order are not doing their job properly. The Chinese tend to think both reasons apply—a sobering thought.

A bloody crime in Beijing in 1994 brought to light the incompetence of the police when it came to facing down killers and bank robbers rather than roping in wayward dissidents. A deranged soldier with an assault rifle opened fire, killing ten people, including an Iranian diplomat and his children, before being gunned down himself by policemen. The police simply were unable to make a quick decision from among the possible strategies for neutralizing the maniac. Beijing residents already knew that the police were corrupt; this tragedy, which took place before their eyes, revealed the police's inability to protect them in a real emergency. As for the justice system, it is bound to the political power structure, serving mainly as an instrument of repression. Judicial severity has tended to be seasonal, reflecting the rhythms of various campaigns. During the two years prior to the "strike hard" campaign, the courts were gradually becoming heavy-handed all year round, sentencing hundreds of petty thieves to immediate execution. The increasing recourse to the death penalty betrays the government's impotence, as does the indefinite prolongation of the 1996 campaign. The authorities are striking harder and harder, but somehow they're not managing to stop the rise in crime.

In rural areas, things aren't any better. Highway robbers, gangs specializing in the sale of women and children, and animal rustlers plunder the countryside. THE SITUATION IN TERMS OF LAW AND ORDER IN CERTAIN RURAL ZONES IS BAD. WARLORDS MAKE THE LAW. In newspapers and official reports, these kinds of headlines call attention to the rural predicament. Translation: The Communist Party no longer controls the villages; the new leaders, who are more or less honest, have been forced to come to terms with local gangs. In many areas, Party officials have deserted their posts, giving in to the magnetic pull of the city and abandoning their mission of rescuing rural regions from underdevelopment.

Along with small-scale banditry and political abdication in the villages, there is a renewal of organized crime, dominated by the mainland branches of the Hong Kong and Taiwan triads. Particularly well-established along the coast, these mafia-like organizations are spreading rapidly in the interior to provinces like Anhui in the east, Henan in the center, and Sechwan in the southwest, sometimes with the aid of the Chinese secret societies now rising from their embers. According to the police, these branch operations are at an "early stage" of development, but they are recruiting more and more actively among the tens of millions of unemployed, idle rural youth.

Another trap that ensnares young people, rural and urban, is drugs. The famous Golden Triangle, the prime opium-producing territory in the world, is on the borders of Thailand, Burma, and Laos. Narcotics travel through the sievelike provinces of Yunnan, which borders Burma, and Guangxi, which borders Vietnam. The drugs travel east to Guangdong, then either move on to Hong Kong or are distributed for Chinese consumption. Limited at the beginning of the 1980s to the southern regions, where the poppy is cultivated in small quantities for local, traditional peasant consumption, drugs have now invaded the entire country. People have more spending money, and there are more criminals ready to deal. Drugs no longer simply pass through China; they are penetrating and taking root.

No region is spared, not even provinces such as Liaoning and Heilongjiang to the northwest, about 3,226 miles from the sensitive zones. Local newspapers regularly report narcotics busts, the arrests of dealers, and the dismantling of clandestine laboratories. In the southern provinces that are hardest hit by the drug problem, detoxification centers have been established. Administered by the police or the army, they look more like prisons than hospitals. In the big cities of the north, the treatment is not much better, because of a lack of financial means and qualified personnel.

The victims of the drug trade are many, and their stories are harrowing. Keli was a young father who was admired in his neighborhood. A self-made man, he came from a big, poor family, had little schooling, but went into business selling clothes. Like Zhang the millionaire or Zhou the con man, Keli made it. In three years he had amassed a fortune and won entry to the nouveau riche milieu. There, he met the woman who was to become his wife and the mother of his child. He also discovered drugs. First hashish was good for a laugh, then he used cocaine to show off, and finally he took on heroin, his downfall. He went into debt to feed his addiction and ended up selling everything he owned—including his wife and child. Keli came close to dying several times. Now he is in a hospital, vegetating, supposedly in detox.

Keli, the working-class hero, king for a day, is the perfect symbol of the "Chinese Dream"—the local version of the "American Dream." In China, as in America, the dream can become a nightmare.

What steps has law enforcement taken to fight the drug trade? Once again, the response has been deadly but ineffectual. On World Anti-Drug Day, June 26, several hundred drug traffickers are executed—

mostly small-time dealers who are users themselves. The drug trade continues to gain ground, and the number of addicts continues to rise.

The Chinese people, aware of the rising crime rate and the inadequacy of the police response, are turning to defending themselves, a development that is reflected in the increase in sales of security systems and the popularity of exhibitions of security devices. Men carry electric torches that emit electric shocks of 25,000 volts and use miniature apartment alarms. Women avoid coming home late at night and hesitate to take taxis alone; they prefer to carry mini-canisters of tear gas. The rise in robberies has meant a windfall for those who sell metal fences, reinforced doors, and high-security locks. This collection of fortifications blights the suburban landscape, which is starting to resemble the outskirts of some European cities. The wind howls as it rushes through filthy high-rise apartment buildings in neighborhoods barren of human contact, where social life is reduced to a bare minimum. The noise and activity of the city center do not reach the outskirts, which are desperately, despairingly silent. China's cities have become cities, but they are no longer Chinese. Traditional homes, courtyards, alleyways, and craftspeople will soon appear only in storybooks. A few run-down old neighborhoods still survive, but for how long? The modern city spins its web. Nothing can stop the wreckers, which care nothing for human life. Residents may find themselves miles from their old homes and workplaces, with no public transportation projected in the current five-year plan, nor in the next. As always, the cart's before the horse.

TRANSPORTATION BEDLAM

Since she moved, Yao Hong has become quite a commuter. Every day she leaves home at 6:30 in the morning. Her bike has a derailleur, a significant technical advance reflecting the determined effort of the bicycle industry in China to defy competition from motorcycles and, to a lesser extent, cars. Out of the 460 million bicycles in China in 1996 (how many spokes does that make?), less than half were modern models. But the variety of colors and styles has brightened the cyclist's universe, so long dominated by black paint and uniformity.

Yao Hong pedals to a bus station to catch the seven o'clock bus, which doesn't stop if it's already full. Luckily, in China, "full" means really full—as full as a New York subway platform during a transit strike. Strikes are not permitted in China, but the buses are always crowded anyway. With luck, the professor's daughter catches a subway by 7:30. A twenty-minute ride on the train and a short walk bring her to school by eight. When the weather is nice, she likes to do the whole trip by bike, a good hour in the saddle. But Yao Hong isn't complaining—her daily journey is a dream compared to the nightmarish commutes of some of her colleagues.

The mass transportation problem in China's overpopulated cities will not be easy to solve. Most of the subway projects launched at the beginning of the 1990s in fifteen or so cities have been shelved because of lack of funds. The municipalities realized too late that their budget was insufficient, and the central government has since refused to help the regions, judging that it cannot meet the needs of the entire country. At the municipal level, budgetary problems are compounded by incompetence, which slows development projects when it doesn't compromise them altogether. Most officials just toe the Party line. It is stupefying to compare the speeches and positions of mayors and municipal Party secretaries to those of national leaders—it is as if local distinctions and concerns just didn't exist. Few local leaders take any real responsibility. Young graduates, more alert than their elders and better educated, feel no pull toward public service; they prefer the attractive salaries offered in the private sector.

Internecine battles within the Party also slow down the improvement of the transportation system, leading projects to be either blocked or scrapped; corruption distorts any remaining sense of priorities. So the cities are developing chaotically. A classic example of an incompetent bureaucrat's decision: The entrance and exit ramps from the ring roads around Beijing are placed in the same location. The result: more traffic jams in this city of 12 million, where the four-wheeled empress reigns over pedestrians.

More than a million vehicles were in use in Beijing in 1996, twenty times more than in 1990. When sales of refrigerators and air conditioners take off, everyone applauds. When car sales rise in cities that are unprepared to welcome the heartless convenience of the automobile, everyone groans—even while they secretly dream of saving enough to buy their own car.

To ease congestion in the increasingly crowded center of town, the capital city has established a system whereby small-engine cars and minibuses are allowed to operate every other day. So far, there doesn't seem to have been much improvement in the traffic, since drivers don't follow this directive—it would be hard to enforce it without assigning a traffic cop to watch every car. As for the traffic cops, most of them have never driven a car in their lives; their paychecks are too meager. They quickly become bitter as they watch the luxurious symbols of new wealth rolling down the streets before their eyes. They end up taking revenge by forcing drivers to respect their uniform. The haughty traffic cop signals to a driver caught red-handed violating the traffic laws (which are elastic, to say the least). Imperial on his traffic island in the middle of the intersection, hands in the air regally as he savors his victory, he waits until the perpetrator, already considered guilty, comes scampering up and prostrates himself at the policeman's feet. The cop refuses to meet the gaze of the criminal whose idiot smile begs forgiveness; he lets the victim stew in his own juices while he goes on about his work. Confucius's ghost haunts all of the crossroads in the People's Republic of China.

The traffic cops are careful in selecting their prey; they prefer to stop small cars. Who knows who might be hiding in that black Audi 100 with the tinted glass—maybe it's a Party official? A military figure? An influential businessman? Or, worst of all, a chief of police? Cops would rather squeeze a few coins from the small fry; there are too many risks involved in going after the bigger fish.

Ambitious cops can make ends meet in another way: by selling drivers' licenses. It seems like an obvious idea, but someone had to think of it. Rumor has it that more than half of Chinese drivers bought their licenses. It seems clear enough that there are many self-taught drivers, and they don't mind bragging about having purchased their driving permit.

"Hey, Zhang, got your car yet?" Xiao Li asked his friend during an evening party of young hip artists.

"I'm taking my driver's test in two weeks," Zhang responds, provoking an endless, deafening chorus of laughter.

"Hey guys, Zhang's taking his driver's test," Xiao cries, holding his sides with laughter. "Are you out of your mind? Why didn't you tell me? For a few bills and one good meal, you can get that taken care of."

Any Chinese person who can afford a car, which costs the equivalent of eight years of the average worker's salary, can afford the 3,000 to 5,000 yuan for driving lessons. But why bother? You can buy the license at half the price. "It helps the cops to improve their lives, so they soften up. It's a new kind of solidarity," Xaio Li says facetiously.

Drivers have limited driving skills, policemen limited effectiveness, and carefree pedestrians and cyclists extremely limited knowledge of traffic rules (at best they can distinguish red lights from green ones). Road safety? Never heard of it—not in school, not on TV. A few basic guidelines could reduce the number of accidents and save drivers from the terror of careening continually through an undisciplined but very relaxed crowd. Pedestrians and cyclists stay calm, cool, and collected no matter what the situation. They never panic. A car shoots by, missing them by two inches; they don't even blink. Never having been behind the wheel, they don't have the slightest idea of how long it takes for a car to brake to a stop. They don't understand the danger, so they saunter through the crowded streets and avenues, children clasped in their arms, persuaded that the cars will avoid them as easily as the bikes do.

First prize for obliviousness goes to the pedestrians who cross two-way streets and look only one way. Just one. Never two. Then they cross at a snail's pace. Second prize is awarded to those suicidal pedestrians who dash fearlessly across the ring roads. Honorable mention goes to the cyclists who ride on the wrong side of the road at night, while saving energy by not turning on their bike lights.

It doesn't help that the roads are mediocre, constructed with low-quality materials, and that the cars are generally in bad condition as well. Most cars, even those fresh from the factory, contain at least one defect, since auto workers tend to be insufficiently trained. Once the cars break down, they fall into the hands of mechanics who are in the trade by pure chance, hired because they are friends of the boss, who is himself poorly qualified. If their friend had been a butcher, they would have become apprentice butchers.

Under the circumstances, it is no wonder that traffic is hellish all around the nation. It's sheer anarchy. In spite of the massive explosion in car sales, China still has the smallest total number of cars in the world, but already the country has the highest number of fatal car accidents. Insurance companies are unhappy and street sweepers refuse to risk their lives cleaning the biggest thoroughfares. For once, no one blames overpopulation, which is not the true culprit. Rural roads are rarely crowded, but the danger there is constant as well, largely because of the pitiful condition of worn-out and overloaded cars, buses, and trucks. A classic news item: "Minibus veers off the road and plunges into a ravine, 30 dead. The vehicle had 19 seats and was carrying 39 passengers. The driver was a novice." Every year tragedies occur as a result of passenger ignorance of safety risks and transport companies' greed. Accidents occur on sea, as well as land. The race for money takes precedence over the safeguarding of human life.

The boom in cars in the city poses another problem that will have to be addressed soon. What about parking? Parking lots are practically nonexistent in city centers and in the new suburbs, except at a few upper-class residences. It may not be long before one quarter of the Chinese people will own a car. It's hard to imagine where they will put them. Some foreign automakers dream of promoting the miniature electric car in China—a shrewd idea.

For the Yao family, purchasing a car is unlikely. The professor is too old to start saving, and his daughter would rather put her money aside for the children. Or rather, the child.

Chapter Six

THE FAMILY IN DISARRAY

In the twenty-first century, words like *brother, sister, uncle, aunt,* and *cousin* will disappear from the vocabulary of most Chinese people. In the land of the only child, the only words you'll need will be *son, daughter, father, mother, grandfather,* and *grandmother*—and, if you're lucky, *great-grandfather* and *great-grandmother.*

The family unit has been dramatically transformed by Deng Xiaoping's drastic birth control measures. The effect is as significant as the outcomes of his economic reforms. Intended to limit the population to 1.3 billion people by the year 2000 and to 1.6 billion by 2050, the program restricts urban couples to one child and rural couples to two or, in exceptional cases, three (when the second is handicapped, for example). The government says that this policy, which has been in effect since the beginning of the 1980s, has prevented 300 million births. Sterilization and abortion are the primary methods of birth control; the government does not promote the pill and the condom, which are considered inefficient and difficult to monitor.

Forty percent of women of childbearing age have been sterilized, and an increasing number of men are following suit. One married woman in four has had at least one abortion in her life. This rate is higher in the city than in the country: in Shanghai, 41 percent of women have terminated at least one pregnancy; in Beijing, 35 percent. In a 1995 study by the Women's Association, 88 percent of women surveyed recognized that abortion had worse consequences on their health than on their reputation. Nevertheless, two-thirds of those responding preferred to keep abortions secret from their colleagues and friends. Abortions are often carried out late in pregnancy and under questionable sanitary conditions. How many Chinese women have lost their lives under such circumstances?

Many young urban couples accept the concept of bearing only one child. A large family would render their tiny apartments unlivable and eat into their modest earnings, cramping their new consumer lifestyles. "There are too many of us," Chinese people always lament. Still, many couples would prefer to decide for themselves how many children they will have. That's the painful part—family planning is coerced. City people, living in close quarters with their neighbors and facing political, social, and economic pressures to conform, find it almost impossible to flout the one-child policy. A few couples have taken the route of public protest, and some have taken their objections to court. They can't hope to win, since the judicial system will not contest laws put in place to enforce political edicts; but at least the couples have the satisfaction of raising the issue.

In the countryside, large families are traditional. So as not to antagonize the peasantry overmuch, the government has granted women the right to bear two children. But rural people see this gesture as insufficient, because many of them find it intolerable not to have male offspring. Chinese peasants say that they prefer boys because they will work in the fields or in rural businesses from an early age and will carry on the family name. The limitation on family size has encouraged the persistence of the age-old custom of murdering baby girls. The infants are usually drowned. There are no statistics about infanticide, but the ratio of the sexes speaks for itself. At the end of 1995, China had 118.5 men for every 100 women. Softhearted families abandon their baby girls instead of killing them, and some money-grubbing parents try to sell their girl children.

Chinese orphanages are overflowing with little girls, as is well-known by foreign couples seeking to adopt. Conditions in these orphanages were examined by the American organization Human Rights Watch. The resulting 300-page report, published in January 1996, stated that every year thousands of orphans die in these public institutions because of staff negligence. The report was based primarily on the damning testimony of a doctor who had worked in a Shanghai orphanage and included horrifying photos of the mistreatment. The Chinese government vigorously contested the findings. Yet the tragic situations of abandoned children must be seen in the context of the current efforts to control population growth.

Rural authorities do not always enforce family planning measures with the same stringency as do their counterparts in the city. Governmental orders are usually recorded on the provincial level, but down at the local level they may not be taken quite so seriously. To a local official, it's all very well for the Minister of Family Planning, Mrs. Peng Peiyun, to affirm that China's survival and the well-being of its people depend on birth control. That's easy for her to say: As everyone knows, she already has several children.

On a fundamental level, what really happens? Slogans on signs and banners warn of massive penalties: ONE CHILD TOO MANY, 50,000 YUAN, TWO CHILDREN TOO MANY, 100,000 YUAN, you may read to your stupefaction as you drive into certain rural villages. But fines of this severity are clearly never applied, and even much smaller penalties are imposed only rarely. Why? Because the village leader is a peasant, too. He belongs to a clan and to a family. He may have a profound belief in the necessity of controlling population growth in his country in order to avoid a catastrophe like that of India; but he does not have sufficient power to impose rules that violate the traditions and desires of his fellow peasants. He cannot turn to the Communist Party for help, since the Party's power in rural areas has crumbled with the dismantling of the people's communes.

Even when a local official has the ability to enforce birth control measures, he may not be motivated to do so. Hopes of securing a promotion for a job well done may be less compelling than the bribes received from families in exchange for turning a blind eye to "illegal" births. All the local leader has to do is fiddle with the statistics, whipping up some flattering figures that are unlikely to be double-checked. Thus demographic indices can be trusted only up to a point.

If a family bent on procreation fails to corrupt the village leader, there's always the possibility of "negotiating" with a doctor who, for a few hundred yuan, can write up a fake sterilization certificate. Where there's a will there's a way. There's some risk involved for the doctors; a handful of them have been sentenced to major prison terms for succumbing to corruption of this kind.

A QUALITY POPULATION

In 1994, national family planning leaders were bolstered by the enactment of a controversial law for "the protection of women and children." Because of the eugenic nature of the legislation, it was adopted only after a year of hesitation, and it was later denounced not only by Westerners but by a segment of the Chinese medical community as well. The text of the law purely and simply forbids the birth of children with mental or physical malformations. According to this law, the choice of whether or not to give birth to a defective child is not up to the parents; it's imposed. The chilling rationale put forward is "to improve the quality of the population," to make "healthy children." How? Through the use of ultrasounds, abortions, and the systematic sterilization of couples in which one member is handicapped, alcoholic, or a drug addict.

Apparently, the Chinese don't know what to do with the handicapped. "They cost society a lot," some say. "There are already enough of us, and we have enough problems," others add. Why would anyone feel a sense of solidarity toward a handicapped person, when there is already so little solidarity among the "normal"? There is a law to protect and integrate the handicapped, but in practice, segregation is the rule. The national association for the handicapped is presided over by none other than Deng Pufang, the oldest son of Deng Xiaoping, who is a paraplegic supposedly because he was thrown out a window during the Cultural Revolution (or, according to another story, because of an accident). But Deng Pufang has publicly announced his support for the "quality population" law. Is this really his personal point of view, or does he just have to help maintain the fiction of the unanimity of the Communist regime?

The Chinese government resents the way the news media and doctors abroad have compared this controversial law to Nazi policies in Germany's Third Reich. Although the legislation was postponed and amended somewhat, it eventually passed with its basic substance intact. Whereas Mao and his associates counted on "quantity" to get China out of underdevelopment, his successors want "quality." Neither regime bothered asking the opinions of parents; individuals are expected to subordinate their interests to the national good. One clear danger of the increased emphasis on the prevention of birth defects is that ultrasound can also be used to detect the sex of the fetus, so babies whose only handicap is their sex can also be eliminated.

THE ONLY CHILD

Not every little girl is unwanted. Ning Ning, born in 1990, is the only child of Yao Hong, and the beloved granddaughter of Professor Yao. She's a healthy little girl, chubby and lively as the dickens. She knows, or will soon know, that she will never have a brother or sister. That's just the way it is. So she won't have to learn how to share her toys; she's not so good at that anyway. She's the most beautiful, the most intelligent child—the head of the household, respected and obeyed by all, the capricious conductor of her own family orchestra. If Mom or Dad try to veto her plans, Grampa steps in with an override: "Ning Ning said..." Whatever happened to the idea of unconditionally obeying one's elders, supposedly a cornerstone of the Chinese character? It's been turned around; now elders kowtow to the little ones.

Professor Yao knows he's spoiling the child, but he can't stop; it would ruin his own pleasure. He's very happy. He's taking revenge on history, making up for the hardship and hunger he, his wife, and their two children had to endure. His first wife died from lack of adequate medical care. His children are far from robust: calcium, vitamins, and protein were all cruelly lacking when they were growing up. To heck with killjoy sociologists and ignorant doctors! Ning Ning's going to get what her parents and grandparents never had: good, rich food, buckets of toys and games, outings to the most modern and expensive parks, pretty clothes, and the best education that money can buy in Beijing. "You only live once, and I want to give her the best chances. What's wrong with that?" Yao Hong says. "It's expensive for us, of course, but we don't feel that we're depriving ourselves. When we decided to give her piano lessons starting at five, my father jumped with joy. He didn't even ask us how much it would cost, even though we're not exactly rolling in money."

What future awaits this overprotected generation, raised in an overflowing bubble bath of excessive happiness? These children, constantly surrounded by helpful grandparents and parents, tend to be self-centered and lacking in courage. They seem ill prepared for a society based on the principle of survival of the fittest. Unlike their parents, these children have lived in relative abundance (or some have), and they have no odious and humiliating past to make up for. Perhaps their arrogance and selfishness will come in handy when they start to assert themselves and take responsibility for their lives.

There's another potential danger in the extreme attention lavished on the only child. Parents who have spent enormous amounts of money on their children in the first years of life may expect to be rewarded by their child's scholastic achievement later in life. This obligation from the child to the parent is much stronger in China than in the West, and the school system is one of the most rigorous and most selective in the world. Competition among students, designed to create elites, is compounded by social competition among families afraid of losing face. The pressure can lead to tragedy: Newspapers frequently report on suicides by students, even among very young pupils, who failed an exam or were simply afraid of their parents' rage at their bad grades.

While young, the only child reigns supreme. This is true in all social classes. Ning Ning isn't from a wealthy family, but her life bears a strange resemblance to that of Zhang Donghua's son—give or take a couple of hundred yuan a month. The style of child rearing and the behavior of the children are identical in these two families. Rich or poor, the only child lived like a prince even before the economic boom. The reduction of the family unit came about at the same time as the rise in the standard of living—and the only child was promoted from prince to emperor, ousting the elderly family members.

RESPECT YOUR ELDERS?

Today's youth no longer seem to follow the Confucian code of unquestioning obedience to the elderly. There's still a vague idea that fathers and paternal grandfathers should be respected, but that's it. A Chinese youth reaching adulthood in the 1990s, brought up on American films and videos, may well know more about Michael Jackson than about Confucius. Young people keep their eyes open, watching the whole world.

A few years ago, people still spoke of sacrificing their jobs for their families. That's when jobs were assumed to pay miserably and, in any case, were not freely chosen. Now it's assumed that you might find actual satisfaction on the job. You might enrich your spirit and also fill your pocketbook. So you're working for yourself, not for your parents and even less for your country. The family has to adapt to these new attitudes. Furthermore, young people are less and less in a hurry to start their own households.

In the interests of birth control, the law sets the minimum age of marriage for women at twenty and for men at twenty-two. This law has met with little opposition in the city. In rural areas, some families still marry off their children at early ages. But young peasants are neither as docile nor as isolated as one might think; they are more and more influenced by ideas of independence. The mobility of the rural population and the development of towns have profoundly transformed family behavior. Ideas of freedom crisscross China, spreading through city and countryside.

The traditional image of a Chinese household featured three or four generations living in harmony under the same roof. Now people admit that this sunny picture is about as realistic as that of workers and peasants joyfully working forty-eight hours a week for peanuts in people's communes. True, as long as there's a housing shortage and pitifully low salaries, there might well need to be three generations living under the same roof. But as for harmony ... Chinese literature and cinema abound with stories of the quarrels, shattered families, tyrannical mothers harassing their daughters-in-law, wives denouncing their husband's faults to parents, and so on.

Differing conceptions of how to relate to one's elders led to a problem in the Yao family. A stormy debate pitted Professor Yao against his brother and sister concerning the possibility of putting their father in a retirement home. Over eighty, the old man was living with his daughter and had become more and more dependent on those around him. The professor considered the retirement home an ideal solution since none of the children were available to take care of their father, and live-in help is hard to find. "He would have been happy in a home, and our life would have been easier, you have to admit it. It was the best solution for him and for us," Professor Yao says. He sees no shame in parents living separately from their children if there are institutions that are decent and can provide appropriate care to meet their needs. The grandfather passed away before any decision was reached.

Retirement homes in China are rare and expensive. There is tenacious resistance to the idea of "placing" one's parents in a home. "It's not our tradition to put old people in homes, like in the West," the Chinese say. What they don't realize is that it wasn't traditional in the West either until more recently. Retirement homes came about through social evolution and the transformation of the demographic landscape—phenomena similar to those occurring, albeit more quickly, in China today.

THE GRAMPA AND GRAMMA BOOM

The population of China is aging rapidly. Those over sixty numbered 110 million in 1995 and will number 135 million in 2002, 230 million in 2020, and 410 million in 2050—one quarter of the population. A grampa and gramma boom. Who will take care of them? Who will pay for their retirement? It's hard to say.

In 1995, only the 30 million elderly living in cities received a pension. The 80 million rural elderly depended entirely on their families. At the present time, most old people can count on two or three children to take care of them. In the twenty-first century this will no longer be possible. Considering the low level of pensions and the high level of inflation, the financial support of children turns out to be indispensable if older people are to live decently. The tendency is to restrict social subsidies and to create private old-age insurance systems, financed by the beneficiaries. (A Chinese newspaper reported that in September 1996, one young couple in Hunan Province named their newborn "Insurance" in honor of the 600 yuan they placed in a special fund which would pay the child 300 yuan per month when the parents reach sixty.)

The aging of the population, due to increasing life expectancy and decreasing family size, is a well-known phenomenon in developed countries as well. In China, however, the economy is still developing. The gross national product is no more than the equivalent of $1000 per person. Taking care of the elderly is going to be a real dilemma for the political leaders of the next century. The government knows it has to act now (although increasing economic disparities between regions make it hard to develop a single national policy). Even if unemployment is minimal in the next century, the working population will never be able to support this oversized retirement-age population. At the family level, in most cases, one child can support his parents—but he'd better be healthy and get along with his parents.

Like it or not, the youth in Maoist times respected their parents more than do the youth of today. Family solidarity was stronger then. The desire for independence was not so preeminent. The young now thirst for freedom—a thirst that they can quench, as long as they're careful.

SEXUAL VERTIGO

Flashback. After the founding of the Communist regime in 1949, individuals were expected to consecrate their energy to building socialism. Therefore, they were expected to reduce their amorous frolics to the bare minimum required by nature to produce the next generation. Mao in person dictated the rules of the game: A couple should not make love more than once a week. (The Chinese were to learn, decades later, that in his Beijing palace the Chairman indulged in lovefests with hand-picked peasant girls.) The Communists forbade the publication of erotic books, contemporary as well as classic, like the famous *Rou Pu Tuan* (*The Pleasures of the Flesh*), which is part of the Chinese cultural heritage, and the well-known works, *Dream in the Red Pavilion* and *On the Shore*.

Today trends are changing. Radio talk shows deal with sexuality, and the Chinese people speak with candor about their desire for satisfactory sex lives.

Confucian-Communist modesty had made adultery a taboo subject; now it's suddenly up for debate. In 1995 the Chinese version of the American novel *The Bridges of Madison County* appeared and immediately became a bestseller. The film based on the Robert Waller novel, which Clint Eastwood produced and starred in, came out in China in the spring of 1996. The debate was immediately revived: Is adultery acceptable in Chinese society? Newspapers echoed popular opinion, suggesting that men and women in the Deng era no longer condemn sex before marriage as, sincerely or hypocritically, their elders did.

Despite the relaxation of media censorship, erotic art and literature are still forbidden. Those who are curious about or devoted to hard-core films and books have to meet their needs secretly. "Can you get me a yellow film?" Chinese people ask their foreign friends—yellow being the color associated with sex. The prohibition and the need for secrecy profits the merchants of sex and pornography.

What about homosexuality? The silence that surrounded this Western-style "depravity" after 1949 has been broken, but without any help from the press. The repression suffered by homosexuals was first of all based on Confucian morality. Communists considered homosexuality to be either a contagious illness to be eradicated or an abnormal behavior to be cured. Homosexuals today are no longer locked up in prison or psychiatric hospitals, but they find it extremely difficult to live openly. On World AIDS Day, a courageous minority of homosexuals came out publicly, distributing brochures about AIDS prevention on the street. But most gays and lesbians have to live out their social lives secretly. They meet in parks at dusk, as unmarried heterosexuals once did (and some still do, if they're too broke for hotel rooms). There is no frank literary treatment of homosexuality. The only film about the subject, an independent production shot by the nonconformist filmmaker Zhang Yuan in 1996, was financed by foreign producers, and it is unlikely to be distributed in China in the near future.

Chinese people have difficulty admitting the existence of homosexuality. In 1995, first in Beijing and then in other cities, a modern French ballet told a story of amorous passion between two men. The audience responded with sarcastic quips, chuckles, and loud remarks about decadence and immorality. Of course, it's hard to tell if the spectators were really shocked, or if they simply felt they had to conform with what everyone else around them was doing.

With certain understandable reservations, educated Chinese are entering a phase of exploring sexual behaviors, as evidenced by the success of the transsexual dancer Jin Xing. Her show played all through 1996 to crowds more interested in the self-expression of a man-become-woman than in modern dance per se. In Beijing, the authorities even sent representatives to the premiere.

There are other indications that things are loosening up. Sex shops have been allowed to open their doors and sell aphrodisiacs, cures for impotence and frigidity, vibrators, and advice books on how to have a better sex life. According to the owners, the products sold in such boutiques as Beijing's Adam and Eve are strictly of medical use (which might lead one to ponder the medicinal qualities of the vibrator). It's true that sexy lingerie, sex toys, and pornographic videos are not to be found in Chinese sex shops—at least, not in the decent ones.

Young people seem to have assimilated some Western notions of sexuality, and at the same time they are returning to Chinese sources of pleasure that Maoism had tried to discredit. Some give themselves over wholeheartedly to promiscuity without taking into account the dangers, such as the risk of AIDS. But little by little, secondary schools and universities are introducing sex education.

Young people are finally coming to see love as a source of physical pleasure and not merely as the hypothetical consequence of a marriage, often arranged, as puritanical Chinese Communists had led them to believe. Sun Lin denies that there has been any evolution, but at least she's willing to talk about the subject, which shows some openness. "In the country if a girl is suspected of premarital relations with a man, she won't find a husband, and that's the way it should be," she says, blushing a little. "Men and women should be pure before marriage," the little peasant goes on, immediately hiding her mouth in her hands like a child who has said a silly thing. Xiao Bai, the concubine, has a different opinion: "The young are starting to taste pleasure; it's fabulous, and it makes them more responsible. They can marry if they want to, with a better knowledge of their partners.... Before, our parents and grandparents married without love. The result on the emotional level was catastrophic, and adultery was very widespread, although it was little discussed, because it was one of those things from which socialism protected us. Some protection!" She bursts into laughter.

Chapter Seven

THE IRON HAND IN THE VELVET GLOVE

A foreign visitor to China is first of all struck by the economic dynamism, the rapid rise in the standard of living, and the outward appearance of consumer happiness. But it doesn't take long to discover what lies beneath this energetic and pleasure-hungry veneer. Fear lurks in every alleyway where the "secret" police—though their existence is hardly a secret—take care of the dirty work. Their task is to protect a system whose survival depends on repression.

To be sure, the Chinese have certain liberties. They spend their money as they please. They can set up businesses if they play the game of corruption and plow through the endless bureaucratic forms. They can travel freely to the interior of the country, and millions of them travel abroad every year, on business or privately—a passport is no longer a reward for the Party faithful. All of these freedoms are important. On the eve of the year 2000, the Chinese enjoy real individual liberties.

But one form of liberty remains out of reach, out of respect for the sacrosanct stability of the nation: freedom of expression. It is impossible for a Chinese person to say or write publicly what he or she believes. It is impossible to formulate aloud any criticisms of the Communist Party without risking a stint in prison. When a revolt gains momentum, there's always the army, ready to fire on a defenseless crowd of protesters, as they did in 1989.

The Chinese Communist Party has never received a mandate from the people it governs. Since 1949 it has held power based on violence. Even before "liberation," life in the Communist-controlled zones was no joking matter. Opposing views were not tolerated at that time, and any "adversary" deemed dangerous was physically eliminated. This brutal system was carried out on a larger scale after the founding of the People's Republic. Many Chinese people believed the new system would be a utopia, where the people, freed of the exploitative yoke of a cruel and corrupt nationalist regime, would reign. But they were the victims of false advertising. The people were swindled in 1949, just as they are today in the stores of the socialist market economy, where the shelves are stocked with fake brand-name products.

NOT READY FOR DEMOCRACY

The handful of men clinging to power in Beijing today insist that democracy would lead to chaos, suffering, and misery. This scenario is plausible enough to dissuade many Chinese from actively opposing the regime. Nevertheless, one might ask, what about the suffering and misery already inflicted on the population in the name of socialism? The list of horrors is long, from the purges of the 1950s to the Tiananmen Square massacre, including the Great Leap Forward, the Cultural Revolution, and other less-well-known but equally bloody campaigns.

The superiority of Chinese socialism over other systems of government is taken for granted by the authorities. According to them, the official rating for Maoism is "70 percent positive." These statisticians are surely hoping to break this record in the post-Mao era—although as long as socialism remains the official ideology, they'll probably have to let Mao appear to come out a little bit ahead in any comparisons with Deng.

For millions of Chinese people, material life is indisputably better today than it was under Mao. Wouldn't it be better still without the Communist Party? Why should a tyrannical few refuse to grant freedom to more than a billion people? Isn't withholding this right likely to plunge the country into a new tragedy? Those in power refuse to consider these questions. They stick to that old refrain, beloved by all autocrats: "The people aren't ready for democracy." Have the people ever been asked their opinion? No, of course not; that would be too risky. Intellectuals thought their opinions were being solicited when Mao launched the "100 flowers" campaign in 1956. They thought they were free to criticize the functioning of the regime in order to help avoid the hardening of socialism. This little breeze of democracy was swept away in a hurricane of state violence directed against those who had spoken out too loudly.

Astoundingly, the regime finds international support for its argument that a population that lacks sufficient education is not ready for democracy. Chiming in with this hackneyed refrain are certain Western "democrats," "friends of China" (but no friends of the Chinese people), and other sycophants of the regime, who are motivated by mercantile concerns. Pray tell, what level of education magically makes people "ready for democracy"? How much schooling does a Chinese person have to have before he or she can cry "Down with the Communist Party!" without ending up with a bullet in the back of the neck?

The regime's argument is further weakened by the leaders' own claims that illiteracy has been nearly eradicated. There is no justification for withholding democracy—it is a universal human right avowed in an international charter endorsed by China. China seems unembarrassed by this fundamental contradiction, but then, the country doesn't bother to enforce its own laws (except the most repressive ones), so why worry about international conventions? When challenged, the government justifies its actions by invoking Chinese "specificity"—meaning that the values of China are different from those of the rest of the world. Some major powers accept this argument, or cynically pretend to, in order to secure profitable trade contracts. (These contracts are supposed to preserve jobs in the developed countries. Although this may be true in the short term, for many Western companies the middle range goal is to delocalize production, closing factories and reopening them in China where labor is cheap. Democracy is of no more importance to the heads of multinational companies than it is to Chinese leaders.)

The Chinese people, supposedly too uneducated to appreciate democracy, have another damning fault: They've never known democracy. The power elite, ensconced in their apartments in Zhongnanhai, apparently are convinced that Confucius is still going strong after 2,500 years. Thanks a lot, Confucius. Thanks for teaching respect for the rules of nature, for the rule of the family, for the ruling class. "We're right to revolt!" Mao said to the hotheads of the Red Guard at the beginning of the Cultural Revolution. (This slogan must be part of the negative 30 percent of Maoism!) At that time, Confucius was held responsible for all of the misfortunes of China (although his authoritarian principles still served). Since then, the philosopher has been rehabilitated. He's a hit with political leaders and with certain intellectuals who emphasize the concept of respect for the established order, emptying the ancient philosophy of its religious content.

"Market socialism" has cashed in on this restoration of Confucius. The little town of Qufu, Confucius's birthplace, has been transformed into a tourist trap. Money is the only thing respected here. Souvenir shops, snack bars, restaurants, rickshaw rides—anything to cash in on Confucius's name. "It's not an unpleasant place, but you wonder where you are," Professor Yao said after a visit to Qufu. He went there during a university conference—one of those meetings during which participants spend three-quarters of their time touring, wining, and dining for free. "In some ways, Qufu reminds me of Shaoshan." That's the birthplace of Mao, in the southern province of Hunan, where the souvenir business also reigns supreme.

A third argument is put forth by the government to justify its rejection of democracy: Many regions are economically underdeveloped. Apparently a poor peasant is capable of enough understanding to "vote" for the only Communist candidate on the ballot but totally baffled by the idea of choosing among several. No, you wouldn't want to put democracy in the hands of just anyone. The real problem faced by the regime in underdeveloped regions is that granting democratic rights might reveal the hostility of poor people to the officials and tax collectors who are destroying them. The regime's arguments have a terrifying "logic," which suggests that the dissidents are right: The Party fears the people—and is used to treating them like cattle. Cattle to be fed.

For the last of the regime's arguments against democratic rights is that the right to food, clothing, and shelter must take priority in China. No one questions the Communist achievement in these areas—even if propaganda has exaggerated the victories and hidden the defeats. Mao made sure that the people of this overpopulated country had something to eat when they were hungry. But what foundation can there be for the argument that the right of freedom of expression is incompatible with the right to eat? What's wrong with talking with your mouth full? Furthermore, today, while members of the elite are eating and drinking to their hearts' content, a greater and greater segment of the population lives precariously, poverty is far from eradicated, and the educational and public health systems are deteriorating. More and more Chinese people fear that the ruling totalitarian system will not be able to guarantee the fundamental right to subsistence.

"What kind of government could lead such a vast and populous country without any problems? None. But by insisting on giving the market economy a greater and greater role without loosening the political system, the Communist Party has made an error. It's going to be hard to get out of the trap," one dissident declares. Another remarks that the Confucian model is less and less able to maintain order and stability as the economic stakes rise. "Confucius's idea was that respect for the family should prevail over respect for the prince. As long as the country was very poor, it was easy to maintain the people's submission to the Party. Internecine feuding within the power elite was limited to struggles for political power. Today, money has twisted the minds of everyone and changed the rules of the game. Money makes a mockery of authority. Corruption is widespread. The children of high leaders, known as 'the little princes,' are struggling not for ministerial posts but for positions as the heads of companies, or for juicy investments, or for a stock portfolio. Political alliances are crumbling, money rules, the situation is degenerating."

Political power today depends on economic power. The ideological vacuum is unprecedented in modern China. In the Maoist period, activists and officials subscribed to noble ideals of social justice; they were fighting for a better society. Now the dictatorship rests on no principles at all. Political commitment is dead. Chinese socialism has gone bankrupt, but its bosses refuse to step down. The goal of those in power is simply to stay in power and enjoy it—not to move toward Communism. The party in power is still called "Communist," but you could just as easily call it "Populist" or "Nationalist"—it would make no difference.

INDOCTRINATION AND CENSORSHIP

Today, as in the past, Chinese totalitarianism works through indoctrination, starting with little children. Kids learn that their country is the center of the world, that it has the oldest civilization, that Mao and Deng were exceptional human beings, that one must love the Communist Party and the country (they go together). Schoolteachers don't necessarily believe all this, but they don't dare state their opposition publicly; they're afraid of losing their jobs. The teacher's role is not to awaken but to silence the critical thinking and imagination of children, to stuff them with lies that they will then parrot for their nine compulsory years of schooling (if they stay in school that long).

Go to school, raise the flag, sing the national anthem in the school yard. The Pioneers, decked out with their eternal red scarves, learn to march in step, braying slogans without understanding a word of what they're saying. Every Chinese child is a Pioneer from the age of seven until, in adolescence, he or she "chooses" whether or not to join the Communist Youth League. Membership, in theory voluntary, is effectively obligatory in cities where the Party remains well organized. But the doors of paradise are closed to morons and nonconformists. You have to deserve to belong to the League. Yao Ding, the professor's son, was never granted that honor. "I was the only black sheep in my class," he remembers. "I had good marks, but the teachers didn't like my attitude—or maybe they just felt they had to pretend they didn't. Long hair, shirt not tucked in—it didn't go over very well. They even called my father in once."

The Chinese love TV, and the Pioneer spirit is there, too, pouring out of the little screen. In between the violent Japanese cartoons there are propagandistic "games" and "stories" serving up the same hash the kids get at school: love of country, love of Party. These "youth programs," crammed with lies and distortions, do not rival the popularity of the cartoons and other lighter, less political shows. The government has repeatedly called for the creation of Chinese cartoons with patriotic heroes defending socialist values and defeating counterrevolutionaries.

The regime's task is difficult: to educate an elite capable of meeting the economic challenges of the twenty-first century, while preventing the development of the critical intelligence necessary for a citizen to become a real social activist. The brainwashing affects everyone, from age seven to seventy-seven. "One phrase can make a country great, one phrase can ruin it," Confucius said—and the Communists have heeded his warning. China is one of the rare countries on this earth that does not have even one free newspaper, out of tens of thousands of newspapers. Literally millions of copies of daily papers are printed daily, just to preach the same hollow sermons. A young journalist starting out at the official New China News Agency (whose president must be a member of the Central Committee with ministerial rank), learns right away that his or her loyalty must be to the Party. "You're not supposed to investigate and inform; you're supposed to recopy directives. You have to play the game or find another job," one of them explains. "The situation's absurd: in the context of the system of responsibility that has been applied to the public sector, the state asked the agency to make profits to ensure its own development. So you see the main spokesperson for the regime rushing about investing in real estate, hotels, restaurants, just like any press magnate in a capitalist country—and all the while he's publishing litanies to the glory of socialism."

After thirty years of transmitting Mao's thought, the press now disseminates the theories of Deng and his successors. All key posts in the press organizations are held by Party officials specializing in disinformation. The top position is that of the powerful Propaganda Department of the Central Committee, which supervises all forms of communication—political, cultural, and journalistic.

From the public's point of view, the result is wretchedly dreary. The leading news stories—whether written, spoken, or broadcast on TV—are inevitably about the activities of top leaders. Ninety-nine times out of a hundred, there is nothing interesting about these activities: visits to factories, visits to farms, meetings with model workers, scientists, soldiers, the old, the young, the handicapped, the old handicapped, young soldiers, model scientists ... followed by reports on the promising economic situation and the no-less-glorious successes of the latest "campaign." All of this is presented without any independent analysis. If you compare the major dailies of the mid-1990s with those of twenty years ago, you'll find no fundamental change. There are only cosmetic changes—but the social transformations under way are more profound than a face-lift. The slogans of today are different, contradictory, but they have one characteristic in common with earlier slogans: They ring false.

Only in economic news reporting has there been any real change. But at the same time, the press's attempt to pay greater attention to economic matters is hampered by the fact that most of the statistics that are reported are faked. This is according to experts—even government experts. The inaccuracies are not the result of mistakes made by statisticians; they are manipulations made by local officials who fiddle with economic statistics for the same reason they doctor demographic statistics—to make themselves look good to the central authorities. The consequences for the country are serious: There is no reliable information on matters as important as agricultural production and economic inflation. People have no confidence in official indices of inflation; they're sure that official figures are well below the real ones. The government has adopted a law to punish those who doctor the figures, and Beijing puts all the blame on provincial authorities, although national leaders also downplay problems when doing so suits them.

The Chinese system of media control works so well that censorship prior to publication is nonexistent, at least in theory. Self-censorship is enough. The specter of being accused of the crime of *lèse majesté* haunts all editors. As for journalists, if they should ever forget their duties, the government reminds them: The Propaganda Department sponsors national meetings, and the government imposes jail time on offenders who are caught. The journalist Gao Yu, for example, was sentenced in November 1994 to six years in prison after a sham of a trial that was carried out behind closed doors. Gao, age fifty at the time of sentencing, had been arrested the year before when she tried to leave the country temporarily to study at the Columbia School of Journalism in New York. She was charged with divulging "state secrets"; in reality, the regime couldn't tolerate her contributing to the Hong Kong magazine *Mirror Monthly*.

Journalists who want to report information rather than propaganda look for cracks in the system: ways to discuss or denounce social problems in a disguised manner. This writing-between-the-lines is dangerous, and in any case it is no way to raise the really important issues. Jiang Zemin, the Chinese president, is aware that the new generation of journalists leans toward reform. His response is to make pronouncements, solemnly warning that the media must "remain firmly in the hands of people loyal to Marxism, the Party, and the people" and must "respect the political line" in order to feed it to the public.

Calls to order by the authorities have become more frequent since Beijing Spring, which revealed the thirst of the citizenry for information and the corresponding desire of journalists to disseminate it. Many journalists demonstrated at that time, under their own banner. Afterward, some quietly returned to their jobs, while the unlucky ones went off to jail. At the height of the 1989 movement, the press reported events with unheard-of candor, made possible by the anarchy reigning in high state circles. It was wonderful to see the pleasure with which the people of Beijing devoured the press during those days of wildness and dreams. Even the television stations got into the spirit of the times. No one can forget the televised debate between student hunger strikers and Prime Minister Li Peng, aired live and rebroadcast later—evidence of the incredible freedom state television had during the last days of May 1989. Now a tape of the debate is a collector's item. The verdict of public opinion is that the students won hands down, managing to ridicule the man who was to establish martial law a few days later, the man whose name would be linked forever with the massacres that followed. This debate was the only real democratic exchange that has been aired on TV in the history of Communist China—and it happened on the eve of tragedy.

Today no Chinese person in his or her right mind reads the major official newspapers like the *People's Daily.* Nonetheless, every day several copies of these papers are shipped to tens of thousands of public institutions and companies. The official dailies aren't sold in the street. "Ask a news vendor for the *People's Daily* and he'll look at you as if you came from the moon—or he'll run away—or he'll punch you in the face," jokes Zhang Donghua. It may seem hard to believe that no one reads a newspaper with a print run of 5 million. What about in the public sector, where people receive it for free? Well, it makes a good fan in summer for those who work in buildings without air-conditioning, and it's an excellent crumb collector all year round (the Chinese love to snack anywhere, anytime). At most, the paper is read by officials who use the editorials to prepare their speeches. It's an amazing waste of paper and ink. China publishes several national papers, printing more than a million copies of each. And every region and city, large and small, has at least one Party daily.

Readers snub the national press; instead, they read small local newspapers that cover social events and crime in detail, and they buy specialized magazines. Kiosks are crammed full of all kinds of publications that the Chinese people read for amusement. Like most of his compatriots, Zhang Donghua doesn't read any of the political dailies; his business subscribes to official economic magazines and newspapers so that members of his company can discern the government's plans and anticipate both positive and negative trends. Zhang knows that subscribing to an official paper is well looked upon by the political figures to whom a businessman may have occasion to turn. For pleasure, Zhang reads the weekly *Football*—a sport he's crazy about. Professor Yao regularly buys the *Beijing Youth Daily*, run by the local branch of the Communist Youth League; it has a snappy tone that breaks with the heavy-handed propaganda of the national press. This paper and the *Beijing Evening News*—a rag full of road-killed pandas and TV listings—are the most widely read papers in the capital. The *Beijing Youth Daily* even has readers in the provinces, an unusual phenomenon for a local paper.

The professor listens to the Chinese shows on the BBC, Voice of America, and Radio France Internationale. Thanks to these foreign programs, which sometimes can't be heard because of government jamming, the Chinese do not live in the state of total ignorance that the regime desires. Xiao Bai never reads official propaganda. She sometimes leafs through *Beijing Youth Daily* for the gossip. Her real interest is in women's magazines, such as the Chinese versions of *Elle* and *Vogue*. Sun Lin reads nothing—and not only because she has difficulty reading. "It's not interesting," she says. "It's all lies." Sometimes she casts a distracted glance at the *Beijing Evening News* left lying around by her employer, and she pays some attention to the 7 P.M news. She especially likes the commercials just before and just afterward—they make her laugh, especially when they show peasants, always jovial.

"Serious" weeklies and monthlies, such as literary magazines, are very strictly controlled. They walk a tightrope and are often on the verge of being closed down. The articles have lost the energy that they had in the 1980s, when it was possible for intellectuals to express critical opinions without the powers-that-be seeing them as dangerous firebrands out to destroy the Party. Now any statement of opinion that even hints at or implies a minor criticism of the regime can lead to the firing of the writer and the termination of the publication.

If it weren't for foreign radio and TV received via satellite, more than one-quarter of humanity would be in the dark about the situation in their own country. Through the foreign media, Chinese people get real information—and they dispatch some of their own real information, too. Since 1989, when the screws were tightened on the Chinese press, foreign correspondents in Beijing have often been approached by men and women whose "sensitive" stories have been refused publication in the local press. Most of these stories aren't about state secrets or even about political matters. They may be about judicial problems, conflicts with official institutions, or crime stories implicating official organizations. If the information seems well founded, it is usually picked up and reported in the foreign press. Sometimes the result is a misunderstanding, because the informant may overestimate the influence the Western media can have on the Chinese government, and/or the informant may hope for a little monetary reward in return for the story. Foreign correspondents, for their part, are wary. Closely watched by state security (the secret police), they have little room to maneuver, and they know it. The threat of expulsion hangs over their heads like a Sword of Damocles. Foreign journalists operate under the jurisdiction of the Department of Information of the Ministry of Foreign Affairs, whose officials cultivate a feeling of insecurity by hosting "friendly" meetings in which journalistic limits are politely mentioned, and "advice" is proffered on how to provide better coverage of China. Used to giving orders to "its" journalists, the Chinese government does the same with foreigners—in terms that are vague, but not hard to decipher.

Government spokesmen unblinkingly affirm their respect for freedom of expression, but they say that writing about the People's Republic takes a special touch because of "Chinese specificity"; thus the regime is able to pay lip service to universal principles while blatantly flaunting them. Reporters who covered the United Nations World Conference on Women got a taste of freedom of the press "with Chinese characteristics": conference newsletters put out by participating nongovernmental organizations were delayed or refused publication—a first in UN history. These instances of censorship, as well as other stunts that were, to say the least, undemocratic, did not prevent UN Secretary General Boutros Boutros-Ghali from publicly congratulating the Chinese government for the smooth functioning of the conference.

Encouraged by the flattery or complicit silence of the international community, China carries on with its censorship, including that of the foreign press. If the *International Herald Tribune* publishes an article that the authorities consider unfriendly, the paper disappears from newsstands in China—or rather, from hotel shops, because street vendors are not allowed to sell foreign newspapers. If an American or European weekly prints an "anti-Chinese" article or photo, the pages in question may be torn out, leaving the magazine as ragged as the notebook of a schoolboy trying to hide his bad grades from his parents.

Television has not been spared censorship. In 1994 the government outlawed the installation of satellite dishes used by individuals to receive foreign shows. Today the production, sale, and installation of satellite dishes are theoretically limited because very few permits are granted for their use, but the disks sprouting up on many rooftops suggest that these regulations are often circumvented.

WITCH-HUNT

Chinese people who want to express themselves outside of official channels face ruthless oppression. The tentative process of political reform begun in the 1980s ended in 1989. The witch-hunt came back—with a vengeance. The government has been hunting down and destroying dissident groups and individuals ever since. By the end of 1996, few activists remained at liberty in China. Dissident leaders were languishing in prison or living in exile. The protesters of 1989, who had been arrested and then freed, were almost all imprisoned once again or expelled when they renewed their peaceful public demands for the democratization of the regime and respect for human rights.

In 1993 when China put in its bid to host the Olympics for the year 2000, the government released a few of its political prisoners in an attempt to win points with the international community. Among those released were the two figures emblematic of Chinese resistance: Wang Dan, the student leader of 1989, and Wei Jingsheng, a tireless fighter for democracy and the organizer of the first "Beijing Spring" in 1978-1979. The ploy backfired. China wasn't chosen for the Olympics. And Wang and Wei, after a brief pause for a breath of fresh air, immediately resumed their peaceful struggle: giving interviews in the foreign press, circulating petitions, writing letters to the authorities— challenges their ex-jailers found intolerable.

The two were soon back in prison. Wei and Wang were sentenced, in 1995 and 1996 respectively, to fourteen and eleven years of prison for "attempting to overthrow the government." As part of a bargain struck between Beijing and Washington, notably to make Bill Clinton's visit to China possible, the two dissidents were finally expelled to the

United States. Exile, used more and more by the Chinese government, has two advantages: it satisfies Western demands that political prisoners be "freed"; at the same time, it gets rid of the troublemakers, preventing the development of a real political opposition.

In the legal arena, positive change seems to be more substantial. This is the judgment of legal experts, both Chinese and foreign—and also the opinion of Zhang Donghua, who occasionally has to turn to the legal system to settle business matters. The progress in judicial procedure is mainly a result of the unbounded activity of the National People's Congress. No longer content to rubber-stamp the proposals of the politburo, this legislative body has been proposing legislation and voting it in. Apparently, some leaders want to grant more importance to law in a country that is too often run arbitrarily. Hundreds of regulations in all areas, particularly in the economic sector, have been adopted since 1992, suggesting a movement toward a state of law. Many of the laws voted in in the mid-1990s are progressive, including a law permitting the opening of private law offices, and a consumer rights law, which grants buyers who have been cheated the right to reimbursement.

This progress must be seen in context, however. The judicial system is not independent; it remains subject to the Party's orders. Laws are easily sidestepped by individuals and by the Party itself, which interprets laws as it pleases and eliminates them from the books when it so pleases. Often, and not only in famous political trials like that of Wei Jingsheng, the judicial process is simply an instrument for demonstrating that the government has the means to maintain social order.

Deng's capitalism has not led to the closing of the gulag (although under his leadership the general atmosphere may seem less suffocating than under Mao). Tenacious dissidents are ready to take advantage of any crack in the system, so the power structure tries to make sure that there are no cracks. There's no dialog—acknowledging the dissidents as credible interlocutors would grant them too much importance. Officially they are "enemies of the people" whose activities will be met with repression, lots of repression, nothing but repression; they are "a handful of grumblers," representing no one but themselves.

But how many members did the Communist Party have in 1949? Only a few tens of thousands. Did these revolutionaries represent the people when they seized power by force? The fear that marks their reign today suggests the answer. The Party now has 50 million members. If the Party were truly supported by the majority of the population, would it have to worry about a "handful" of activists? Is this not an admission of weakness—of illegitimacy?

There is no other explanation for the government's relentless pursuit of dissidents who are a far cry from being fanatics or bomb throwers. The treatment of Wei Jingsheng—his fifteen years behind bars, his second arrest and sentencing, and his exile—reveals as much about the regime's anxieties as about its cruelty. What were Wei's crimes? To have called for democracy and to have called Deng Xiaoping a despot. In the late 1970s, that was indeed daring—and clairvoyant.

Wei was a young electrician at the Beijing Zoo, the son of a military man. In November 1978 he started sticking up *dazibaos* on the wall in the Xidan quarter. He was joined by several companions who also felt that their lives had been ruined by the Cultural Revolution. Many members of this "lost generation" hoped that de-Maoization would lead to what Wei called "the fifth modernization"—democracy. (The other four modernizations, promoted by the Communist Party, were industry, agriculture, the army, and science and technology.) On *dazibaos* and in reviews, defenders of Western-style democracy and Marxist critics launched feverish debates. Deng tolerated this exchange of ideas, at first seeing no problem with a movement that reinforced his image as a reformer. Among intellectuals, even Communist intellectuals, there were hopes that the radical economic reforms announced by the little man would be accompanied by a progressive democratization of political life. But once Deng established himself at the top of the state and the Party, he ordered the liquidation of the Democracy Wall, and he imposed heavy sentences on the ringleaders of the movement.

Kill a chicken and scare the monkeys, goes the Chinese adage. In going after Wei, the government hoped to scare other dissidents into silence. But the calculated risk has not been successful—not then, and not now. Just when the government thinks it has destroyed some dissident group, another crops up elsewhere. And the protesters are using the most sophisticated techniques to defy the regime.

The dissidents have discovered communications technology. They are no longer sticking up *dazibaos* and running off pamphlets on grimy machines. Any self-respecting dissident today has a phone (which may be cut off occasionally) or, better still, a cell phone. A fax machine can work magic. This instrument was exploited fully in 1994 and 1995 to circulate petitions about democracy and human rights—until the organizers of the campaign were caught and sent to join those who were already rotting in prison.

Where do the dissidents find the money to pay for this equipment? Most of it comes from abroad, from comrades and support groups. Some Chinese businessmen discreetly help the militants, too. After 1989 many supporters of the democratic cause, and even some activists, set out on the superhighway of business—the only road you can travel freely, where you can go mad, where you can even break the speed limit. As the banking sector developed, the improved infrastructure for depositing, withdrawing, and transferring money made "anti-Party" accounts possible. Occasional police seizures of these accounts are ineffective, considering the Chinese aptitude for money juggling!

Even fax machines and telexes are now becoming old-fashioned: The government's newest enemy is the cyber-dissident. So far, the World Wide Web has primarily served opponents in exile, since the Chinese do not yet have easy Internet access. The few thousand Chinese people hooked up to the Internet live on university campuses—

researchers, professors, and some students. But the network is bound to develop. By the year 2000, there will probably be more than 5 million personal computers in the People's Republic. There is a great future for cyberspace in China. A hundred or so international political organizations already use the Internet, including human rights groups, Chinese dissidents in exile, and Tibetans advocating independence for the Roof of the World.

News may not circulate freely in China, but the thousands of Chinese people living abroad find ways to keep themselves informed and then send ideas back to their country of origin—contagious, politically unacceptable ideas. "The connection to the Internet does not mean total freedom of information," warned the Minister of Post and Telecommunication, Wu Jichuan, in June 1995. His concerns were about political, not pornographic messages. He admitted that the authorities would find it extremely difficult technically to control the Internet. At best, they could try to limit the number of connections and the number of sites—a tough task that is already under way. But total censorship is impossible, as other authoritarian regimes around the world are also realizing.

The dissidents are determined and bold; they have increasing technical mastery and financial means. This in part explains the brutality and the exaggerated sensitivity of the Communist leadership. But there's another reason: The phantoms of Tiananmen Square still haunt the nation. The government is afraid that they will wake; that they will cry out the truth about the "counter-revolutionary riots" of June 4, 1989; that they will incite the people to rise up again at a time when social problems and corruption are increasing. Disunity at the top, because of power struggles in the wake of Deng Xiaoping's death, makes the situation all the more unstable. That is why the government is so paranoid every year on April 5 at the Festival of the Dead, and also on June 4.

These anniversaries are marked by an impressive police presence around Tiananmen Square, around cemeteries, and around the homes of critical intellectuals who are considered dangerous, like Professor Ding Zilin. This woman, whose seventeen-year-old son was killed on the night of June 3-4, 1989, has made it her lifework to compile a list of victims of the massacres and collect the accounts of families who lost a loved one. Before 1989, the professor and her husband were part of the silent majority, dissatisfied but not daring to move toward active opposition, simply trying to lead a life that was minimally bearable and trying to ensure a decent future for their child. The Tiananmen Square massacres led them to dissent. Professor Ding has sworn to continue her struggle as long as she lives, even if she ends up in prison. That is why this woman, who is physically fragile but has admirable mental strength, is so upsetting to the regime. The government arrests her from time to time, knowing that doing so will generate sympathy, but authorities fear that left unchecked her message could become widely known and she could influence a great number of people.

Even the national festival of the Lunar New Year takes place under high surveillance owing to fear of public demonstrations. How can the government serenely affirm that it has things under control and enjoys the confidence of the people? In June 1996, several years after the massacres, the police were still forcing Beijing bookstores to keep lists of clients who used their copy machines!

"I didn't understand when the bookstore owner asked me to write down my name," Sun Lin said after she had gone to make some copies for her employer. "He told me that it was an order of the police and that the policemen would be coming to pick up the list in a few days. Because of 6-4, he told me." (6-4 is the popular name for the Tiananmen massacres, which took place on the fourth day of the sixth month.) The little Henan cleaning lady was all the more mystified because she had only a vague idea about the tragedy that had taken place on the biggest square in the world that warm, gentle spring night years ago. At the time a peasant of sixteen, she had heard only the official version of events: The army had wiped out a band of conspirators and thugs who wanted to destroy the socialist system. She remembers that for several weeks the men in her village were talking about demonstrations and about the occupation of Tiananmen Square. But daily life went on. The drought that year was more worrisome to the peasants than news of the student demonstrations. In this agricultural region where nature shows a cavalier disregard for the human race, people were worried about real hunger—and not because there was a hunger strike. So as the villagers waited for rain to fall on the recently sown fields, they paid only limited attention to what was going on in the capital. They weren't interested in politics—and still aren't.

To tell the truth, politics per se wasn't the main concern of the people demonstrating in the cities. (In eighty-four cities, to be exact. This governmental figure contradicts the official story that the revolt involved "a handful of activists.") Only some of the demonstrators—students, dissidents, and certain politicians—were asking for more freedom and democratization. The majority were mainly concerned about fighting corruption, nepotism, and the rising cost of living. The idea of democracy was conspicuous by its absence. The Chinese were already depoliticized in 1989.

Still, the miracle occurred. The Chinese people, as if astonished by their own courage, confronted the government and made it waver. Of the millions of Chinese people who spat out their discontent and hatred of the government, how many could have imagined a few weeks earlier that they would be able to summon the moral resources to rise up against one of the most authoritarian regimes on the planet? The authorities could hardly believe their eyes and ears. And they learned their lesson. After the massacres they redoubled their efforts to reduce inflation and wipe out corruption. They achieved remarkable success in the first of these projects and total failure in the second. They are trapped in their own system, unable to change it without themselves leaving the political scene—and they won't give up easily. Their only hope is that economic growth and a rise in the average standard of living will save them. They know that they could not survive a second Tiananmen.

The new approach—"you take care of making money, we'll take care of politics"—has placated the majority of the Chinese people. Personal enrichment has given some meaning to lives that until recently had been good and dreary. These days the people are neither more nor less interested in politics than in 1989; they are simply more interested in making money now that that has become a real possibility and not just a slogan. When the government says that stability is indispensable for the pursuit of economic reforms, the people hear them loud and clear. Having seen their purchasing power increase tenfold in recent years, many of the demonstrators who took part in the 1989 uprising will not take the risk of taking to the streets again. But this doesn't mean that the regime has won. The status quo may be convenient, but it is full of unspoken trade-offs, and one thing is perfectly clear to both sides: It can't last forever. "It would be naïve to think that the Chinese have sympathy for their government just because they can consume to their hearts' content," warns Zhang Donghua.

Frank discussions with women and men of every rank and station reveal that the power structure does not have the backing of the people—and is not safe from a new popular revolt. The regime has discredited itself too often. Tiananmen has marked people's spirits forever. If the massacres are no longer discussed every night in the homes of Beijing, Xian, or Chengdu, still, they are not forgotten—not the butchery, not the protest. But people don't want to reopen the wound right now. What good would it do? The divorce between the people and their leaders is complete, but both sides want to avoid a new tragedy.

With this in mind, the government has opened up the economic sphere, giving the Chinese people freedom in this one aspect of their lives. As social problems grow, the government's confidence in its own authority is further threatened. Knowing this, the people are beginning to assert a new sense of entitlement—again, in certain delimited areas.

In the city, as in the countryside, as the numbers of people excluded from the benefits of reform grows, there are more and more matters to protest. There are grumbles of revolt in many regions and in many areas of activity. Nepotism and corruption have not disappeared—far from it—and crime is increasing. Most worrisome is the attitude of businessmen, who are supposed to be the strongest allies of the leadership. Many businessmen owe their riches to corruption. But because of their contact with foreigners, some have come to realize that a certain degree of transparency in institutions is, in the end, the best guarantee of a free enterprise system. In short, democracy sustains the development of economic liberalism. A certain kind of democracy, that is. Young Chinese business owners like Zhang aren't thinking of multiparty politics, but of the legal system and of the equality of each individual before the law. That's what the peasants demand, too, sometimes violently: an end to abuses of power. They want China to become a country ruled by law. The social demands made in the 1990s, whether by the rich or by the poor, resemble those made by the protesters of 1989. In spite of profound socioeconomic changes, the fundamental issues remain the same.

The government, unable to organize a political response to these demands, repeatedly calls for stability and national unity. Rather than addressing how to build a socialist society, government discourse is now devoted to preserving the status quo. There's a paralysis in the political domain. The slightest error could be exploited by a rival faction of the Party; "security" functions at the highest levels, where everyone is spying on the acts and gestures of everyone else. Jiang Zemin, Deng's designated successor, knows that he'll need help from the army if he's to achieve his two-part goal: deepening economic reforms and keeping the political system in place. He's continuing with the life's work of Deng Xiaoping.

THE MAN WHO WOULDN'T DIE

Dear old Deng! He sure kept his heirs waiting. Among his many nick-names there was "the man who never falls," since he kept managing to return to power after being pushed aside. You could give him another nickname: "the man who wouldn't die." In August 1996 the "Little Helmsman" celebrated his ninety-second birthday—a remarkable milestone in a country where life expectancy is about seventy and even more noteworthy since this "appealing tyrant" (as one young dissident called him) was a heavy smoker and a compulsive worker. Deng's main achievement: getting this vast and populous country out of underdevelopment. That was where Mao failed, after he sacrificed millions of human lives in insane attempts motivated by political utopianism. All Chinese people—or almost all—owe much to Deng for having stopped this infernal machine. But the leader's image was tarnished by his lack of democratic vision, confirmed by his intransigence in 1989 and by the move toward unbridled, brutal capitalism during his last years in power. By the end of his long, tumultuous life, people were disappointed with "Little Peace" (*xiao ping*) and his image was not much better than Mao's. The Chinese have already moved on, forgetting the "great architect of reform." His successors, impatient to turn the page, carefully orchestrated his disappearance into oblivion.

Deng retired officially in 1990, at the age of eighty-five, but he continued to pull strings behind the scenes. He had to come out of hiding in 1992 to put an end to the austerity policies that had been in force since 1989. His timorous heirs were slow to resume economic reforms, fearing renewed protests by the people as well as within the Party. But Deng understood that immobility would not satisfy the Chinese for long. Thus during his tour through the southern part of the country, he played his last card: He revved up the motor of the economy, adding new horsepower to the engine. There was an immediate result. The population moved. They were waiting for just that. Now China dreams of being the next great world economic power.

In February 1994 the unseen emperor made his last bow, painfully, before the television cameras. This final public appearance revealed a staggering old man with a haggard face. It was a terrifying vision for a billion human beings who, that evening, realized that the leader was now only a shadow of his former self. Professor Yao remembers: "Everyone was waiting to see the patriarch for a few minutes on TV for the Lunar New Year, as always. Bets were on. What state would he be in? No one imagined a walking corpse. We said to each other, this is it, the post-Deng period has begun. And people started to ask who would replace him. We didn't know. We have no decision-making power. So the only thing we can do is get as much as we can out of life—waiting for we don't know what, we don't know who."

The Chinese people don't expect that the immediate post-Deng years will bring major changes in the way the country is run. It's hard to guess what will happen in the middle term and the long term. Everyone is wondering if Jiang Zemin will stay in power; many are expecting that upheavals are bound to come in the political area, sooner or later. The most optimistic expect an official reevaluation of the 1989 Beijing Spring. Others think that the current repressive atmosphere will not be loosened, since there are too many serious social problems. But there are many men and women who continue to dream of freedom—not just economic freedom, but freedom of expression. And first among them are the intellectuals and the artists.

Chapter *Eight*

THE LION KING AND
THE MONKEY KING

Mao hated the "stinking ninth category"—intellectuals and artists. The son of a peasant, the Chairman was a failed poet; he was jealous of creative people and made it his business to destroy them, whether they were ordinary teachers or famous artists. Joining him in this task was his last wife, Jiang Qing, an actress of mediocre talent but great ambition, who was propelled to the center of the political stage by the Cultural Revolution.

De-Maoization put an end to the systematic persecution of those who think a bit too hard and dream a bit too much. Yet intellectuals and artists remain eternally suspect. The current regime fears that art, like the press, could become a locus for dissent. For the government, proper artists would be like spokespeople, never swerving from the Party line—and, if they should ever have doubts, they would never admit them. Communist-Party-led associations try to control the arts under the guise of promoting them. Writers, painters, and filmmakers invariably sign the rolls of these do-nothing fraternities. Since independent unions are not permitted in China, a group of artists cannot form on its own to reach out to the people.

With regard to artists, the obligatory reference is still Mao's speech ordering them to serve the people and, by extension, to serve the Communist Party. Deep in their hearts, even Chinese leaders know that this speech is a bit out of date—the Discussions on Art and Literature occurred at the Red base of Yan'an in 1942—but to point this out would be counterrevolutionary. The Department of Propaganda and the Ministry of Culture regularly invoke this Yan'an bible perfectly seriously, bringing joy to the hearts of the old-time faithful. "It is necessary to encourage work reflecting the reality of the country and the successes of socialism," intone the officials, who know about as much about culture as Mao did about poetry. In other words, they want socialist realism, in the year 2000. How progressive! But wait—here comes the best part, the really innovative part—they want socialist realism without a penny of funding from the socialist state. The Chinese government is actually asking private and semi-private businesses to finance works whose content will be entirely controlled by the state. They're asking private philanthropists to help transmit Party ideas.

This absurd scheme has emerged from a regime that is engaged in liberalizing the economy but horrified by the notion of liberalizing thought. Yet the government must know that the public cannot be satisfied with a diet that is 100 percent propaganda. So entertainment is allowed, as long as it's inoffensive—which often means that it's idiotic, too.

BROKEN SPIRITS

The nation's cultural policy has turned out to be catastrophic. While money abounds in certain sectors of industry and commerce, culture is the poor cousin of modernization. Private capital goes to organize big shows, touted as examples, but never towards supporting ongoing cultural activities. The quality productions produced each year can be counted on the fingers of one hand—and this in a country of a billion people with a very rich history and culture (as its leaders often remark).

From the end of the Cultural Revolution until 1989, there was some tolerance for artistic audacity. The ensuing burst of creative activity was suppressed after Beijing Spring, reconfirming that art would have to submit to the caprices of politics. Censorship came rolling back. The current leadership is not as ferocious as Mao was; artists who refuse to play ball are no longer sent to reeducation camps. They are pushed into the margins and simply disappear from circulation; or they end up going into business; or they leave the country.

What happens to those painters who aren't satisfied with slapping "The Yellow Mountain Surrounded by Fog" onto a canvas or painting hundreds of pictures of proud harvesters toiling under a radiant sun symbolizing Mao? What happens to the rock bands whose provocative music has attracted capacity crowds? What happens to the writers who have dared to suggest that the concerns of individuals might sometimes take precedence over the interests of the nation? Some hang on, trying to circumvent the censor. Others work at home, hidden from critical scrutiny. Many throw in the towel, tired of struggling against the intransigent successors of Mao and Deng.

In December 1996 two congresses were held, one for artists, one for writers, under the auspices of the Communist Party. It's unlikely that these events improved creative morale, since they loudly reaffirmed the spirit of "socialist civilization." As the *People's Daily* declared in its own inimitable fashion: "The Party must guide artists and writers toward a correct understanding of Marxism-Leninism, Mao Tse-Dong's thought, and especially the theory of socialism with Chinese characteristics of Deng Xiaoping." The Chinese Federation of Arts and Literature elected its new president on this occasion: Zhou Weizhi, eighty years old, a famous composer of revolutionary songs. He is particularly known for his "March of the People's Liberation Army."

Why should artists and intellectuals present a danger to the regime? "Quite simply because we tell true stories, contemporary stories, whereas the government likes stories of the past, false stories, written and rewritten by itself," said one young writer. "Chinese society is experiencing fantastic upheavals, with positive and negative aspects, but the Communist Party can't stand anyone but itself bringing up the contradictions emerging from this new society. It expects us to sing hymns of praise to its policies. If we don't, it is persuaded that our works are arms provided to the people to be used against the Party," adds the writer, who prefers to remain anonymous. His caution illustrates the creative community's deeply rooted fear of being severely reprimanded for making comments that, in a democratic country, would not be considered incendiary. Even the most famous artists censor themselves. How many times, in interviews with the foreign press, have Chinese filmmakers and musicians suggested that "it is preferable" that certain comments not be reported in full? "I'm sure you understand," the fellow then says, resigned, as if ashamed of his knowing air. How can anyone create in this atmosphere of fear and cowardice? Artists are suffocating.

But some artists suffocate in comfort. Dissidents, who take risks continually, sometimes reproach artists and intellectuals who make pacts with the devil. Of course people need to protect themselves, to practice their professions as best they can, but some deals seem a bit too easy—for example, giving up one's principles in exchange for tax breaks. Everyone knows that most movie stars and singers cheat shamelessly on their taxes. From time to time the government throws a fit about it and the press rants and raves against the offenders. It's all an act. The authorities want the artists to be interested in money rather than politics.

"What politics are there?" asks one writer rhetorically. He admits that since the Revolution of 1911, which ended the monarchy and established the republic, literary circles have never been so cut off from political and even social reality. "This is undoubtedly because

China is lacking any ideology, money is making everyone crazy, and our leaders would do anything to maintain power," he says. Even at the height of the storm in 1989, very few stars of the music world or the silver screen openly came out on the side of the students. This marked silence doesn't prevent some of them from "retelling" with many delicious details their stories of Beijing Spring, as if they had had starring roles in a film modestly entitled *Me and Tiananmen.*

No, most of them weren't there, but in the aftermath the Communist Party tightened the screws on the creative professions anyway. This was after a decade of relative tolerance for investigative journalism and even for "the literature of scars," a genre rooted in the torment of the Cultural Revolution. Evocations of this troubled period are still rather well looked upon by the authorities, as long as the works consider only those lives and careers that were broken by the Gang of Four. It is unacceptable to criticize Mao himself, the Communist Party, or the actions of today's leaders back in the days of the Cultural Revolution. The regime doesn't want to take too close a look at this page in the history of totalitarianism. Tightly reined in, writers also risk becoming the unwitting tools of Party machinations. As part of a carefully arranged scheme to eliminate political rivals, a ruling clique may demonstrate its liberalism by authorizing the publication of a "borderline" work. A few short months later, the same book may be declared to be heresy, and the author imprisoned. It would be a miracle, indeed, to see a masterpiece arise from such tortuous conditions.

Wang Shuo doesn't pretend to be writing masterpieces. This prolific young author emerged at the end of the 1980s and quickly rose to notoriety. He's a phenomenon—the only popular author who is tolerated by the authorities. Some of his colleagues call him a wily primitive who has managed to make millions of yuan telling stories about regular people, using slang that no one dared use before. His unsparing portrayals of the lives of young people have plenty to shock even the most reform-oriented leaders; his stories reveal a murky, dismal

China, a dead end for the next generation. But his unique style, often very funny, makes the pill easier to swallow. His works are a delight for readers even if some of them accuse Wang of seeking success at all costs and producing quantity rather than quality, for commercial reasons. The books of Wang Shuo certainly show what political limits can't be crossed. "It's not so bad if you compare it to what my parents used to read," judges Xiao Bai, a wholehearted fan.

Some writers, gathering that the great moment of Chinese literature is not likely to come anytime soon, have packed up their bags and gone to live in the West. That was the decision of Bei Dao, one of the greatest living Chinese poets, a minstrel of liberty whom many consider a possible Nobel Prize winner. Liu Binyan and Su Xiaokang have been exiled since 1989—because they got too involved in Beijing Spring. Liu, a Marxist critic who believed for many years in the possibility of renewing the Party from within, now lives in the United States, where he struggles for human rights back in his homeland—which he will see again only once the current regime has passed away.

Readers don't find much to like in the writings of official pen pushers, or in the work of young writers who are hamstrung by self-censorship. The public prefers books from abroad. In order to survive, publishing companies translate foreign books by the bucketful (without necessarily paying royalties), and they are permitted to publish these works as long as they don't include material that the regime might find offensive. People read romance novels and mediocre detective stories written for the semiliterate and printed on cheap paper.

Meanwhile, the government sticks to its position: The best books are those it commissions. Every year, the press seriously presents the list of prizewinners for best works and bestsellers. In first place, inevitably, are books on political theory by or about Deng Xiaoping or another "old comrade," tales of (revisionist) history, and tomes about the economy. These books fill the bookstore windows; nobody buys them, but they're required to be sent to all "work units." This explains the monster print runs of hundreds of thousands and even millions of copies—enough to make major Western publishers pale with envy.

TREACLE AND SCHMALTZ

The music world has not been spared censorship. In China, music means classical and popular—the government prefers to ignore all other genres—and of the two, popular music predominates. The reason is obvious: Advertisers and sponsors prefer to finance a concert for an audience of 12,000 rather than 1,000. As for the state, it has never invested heavily in training and support for classical music. Budget cuts have even hit traditional opera in Beijing, Shanghai, and elsewhere, although most leaders claim to admire this musical form fervently. The opera no longer has the resources to develop and grow—it has just enough to scrape by.

Opera singers and aficionados are saddened by the loss of their theaters.

Particularly upsetting was the destruction of the oldest opera house in Beijing, located in Jixiang at the heart of the capital, to make way for a pretentious shopping center financed by Hong Kong compatriots, with the blessing of our old friend Chen Xitong, always one on the lookout for a good deal. This music hall had hosted generations of actors and singers, among them Mei Lanfang, considered to be the greatest Beijing opera singer since this type of musical theater came into its own in the nineteenth century. Emotions ran high in an already fragile artistic community that is having difficulty attracting the younger generation. The loss of this institution is a sad symbol of the path China has taken in the cultural realm.

The most lucrative opera performances are those staged for foreign tourists, who can't understand the story (which is complicated by codified gestures) but appreciate the exotic, colorful spectacle, performed by artists who are talented acrobats as well as singers. A few lovely little private theaters, more like teahouses, flourish in big cities.

But the ticket prices are prohibitive for simple opera lovers like Professor Yao, who, not so long ago, used to be able to pay a few yuan to see a show. Affordable culture for the masses is being replaced by folkloric spectacles for those who can pay.

Meanwhile, popular music shows fill the halls, the radio waves, and the TV screens with treacly songs that couldn't possibly give anyone any naughty ideas. Singers willing to warble the same inanities over and over again are generously rewarded for their efforts. "For two or three songs in an evening, I make 15,000 to 20,000 yuan," declares Cidi without embarrassment. She's one of the rising stars of Chinese popular entertainment. "Of course, that's a lot of money, but young artists like us aren't subsidized at all anymore. Our costs are high, we pay taxes, and our careers don't necessarily last very long," explains the singer. "And I've worked hard to get where I am. I make an honest living. There's nothing wrong with it." Cidi believes that her government is doing a lot to improve people's lives. "China has made incredible progress. Let's not just throw stones at our leaders. They're not doing such a bad job."

Cidi sings an average of two songs a night in concerts that feature a dozen or so stars, none of whom has sufficient repertoire to fill an hour and a half. Despite the jovial atmosphere and the banal, innocuous music, the concerts are closely monitored by the police, who prevent the audience from getting up and wiggling at those rare moments when the rhythm picks up. The authorities must be aware of how unpopular they are with the young; they seem terrified that any popular gathering, however inoffensive, might escalate into a full-blown incident. In this fraught atmosphere, rock music, supposedly conducive to uncontrolled behavior, is the symbol of social dissidence. On the average, the authorities authorize only one or two rock concerts per year in big cities—in moderate-sized halls, if possible, so that security measures can be more effective.

Tough luck for the public. The young like rock; they pounce on video clips shown on satellite TV, and on black-market CDs, imported or pirated. Tough luck for the rock groups, too; since the mid-1980s, they've been pouring their energies into reaching their audience. Some of the best rock 'n' roll performers supported the students too openly in 1989. Some of them even played in Tiananmen Square. But the new rock scene was crushed along with nascent hopes for democracy on that famous June night.

Tough luck for the cultural agencies and businesses that dream of organizing and sponsoring big pop concerts bringing together Chinese and foreign stars. Such projects are discussed regularly at Zhang Donghua's club. The money's there. Zhang himself was approached by a friend who specializes in organizing cultural events. Dozens of projects have been proposed to the Ministry of Culture—in vain. It's never the right moment. Impatient Chinese journalists sometimes try to stir things up by announcing the impending arrival of an American star, hoping in this way to force the government's hand. Usually the organizers confirm the project but mention cautiously that the details have not yet been finalized. And that's the end of it.

The regime's antipathy toward rockers has led some frustrated musicians to take up jazz, a genre little known to Chinese authorities or to most Chinese people. Coffee-bar jazz clubs are sprouting up, and the bars of big hotels are eager to host trios and quartets, even inexperienced ones, who can create an intriguing, exotic atmosphere, reminiscent of a Shanghai cabaret in its heyday. The significant advantage of this transition to jazz is that musicians have a chance to make a decent living. Since 1993, Beijing even has its own jazz festival, created not by the public authorities but by foreign residents with the support of their embassies. The Chinese government gave nothing but its approval for this event, whose growing success suggests the curiosity of the Chinese about all new music.

FILMMAKERS' STRUGGLES

China has all the ingredients to produce quality popular cinema and art films: filmmakers with talent and the desire to express themselves, studios with know-how, money, and an audience. But this ideal scenario is ruined by the government's obsession with control. From storyboard to distribution list, the censor is there, snipping and chopping. The public is not fooled; they snub national productions. Movie theaters survive only by showing a few imported blockbusters each year, mostly American, hand-picked by the Film Bureau censors, "thought police" who play it safe and nix most films. They're afraid to make a mistake and have their hands slapped. Better pass the buck to your superior. (No matter what your rank, if you're a bureaucrat, you always have a superior.) Thus a band of fools deprives the Chinese people of the opportunity to see good foreign films, on the pretext that China must protect its internal market and encourage national productions. The real concern is preventing Western "spiritual pollution" into the Middle Kingdom. As if that toxic cloud hadn't already darkened the skies!

As long as the only locally produced films are endless rehashes of the Sino-Japanese War, the public will turn to American blockbusters or pirated videos, no matter the quality. Chinese kids whose parents can afford it enjoy *The Lion King* and *Toy Story*. Too bad they can't see any cartoons made in China. The most famous Chinese cartoon, *The Monkey King*, created in 1962, isn't distributed anymore except on videocassette. This great classic proves that China has what it takes to produce quality films for young people. But the Cultural Revolution sent the cartoonists of the 1950s out into the country to herd pigs, and their successors are not supported by the government.

In an atmosphere of crisis and censorship, what happens to filmmakers? They fall into several categories. First, there are the usual servants of the regime, specializing in historical propaganda films, who let themselves go from time to time and make a lowbrow comedy. Then there are the few talented directors who emerged in the 1980s, people like Zhang Yimou and Chen Kaige, who made names for themselves on the international scene. Last there is the young, post-Tiananmen generation, who insist on depicting the bad sides of contemporary society and who are now being targeted by the regime.

There's no reason to dwell on the official producers and directors whose epic films devoted to the glory of the Party do not attract crowds. As for Zhang Yimou and Chen Kaige, they have started focusing on megaproductions, in contrast to their pre-1989 films. In that golden age, they produced films that evoked, simply and intelligently, the complexity of Chinese civilization. Showered with international rewards, they are now financed by foreign companies. But the government is not entirely pleased about these coproductions and tries to sabotage them. Despite the enormous means at their disposal, these filmmakers have not turned out masterpieces. Their most recent films, poorly distributed in China, have not met with the hoped-for success abroad; they suffer from being the products of a delicate compromise between the desire to evoke the suffering of their country, the recourse to parables and metaphors to get around the censor, and the supposed necessity of seducing Western audiences with garish Orientalism.

The greatest frustration is experienced by young filmmakers whose films almost never come out in China; that is, when they manage to produce films at all. These artists usually operate on shoestring budgets, ten to twenty times less than the budgets of their well-established elders. With help from Hong Kong or Europe, these so-called "sixth-generation" directors remain unknown in their country even as they are beginning to make names for themselves in foreign film festivals.

Zhang Yuan is one of the leaders of the sixth generation. He has been struck from China's official list of acceptable filmmakers, making it impossible for him to use the financial and technical resources of the big state-owned studios. He must make his films independently and try to place them abroad, at the risk of veering toward an art conceived and filmed for a non-Chinese audience. "My greatest sorrow is that my fellow countrymen can never see my films," Zhang Yuan says.

"But I don't have any choice. I have to get into the foreign market and stay there, what else can I do? Otherwise I'd have to start selling clothes or open a bar like everyone else. But I want to keep making films. It's my life." The reasons for the opprobrium he faces? First of all, his desire to treat subjects that the leadership considers sensitive, such as psychiatry, alcoholism, and sexual freedom. Then there's his film *Beijing Hoods*, a raw portrayal of apolitical urban youth drenched in alcohol, sex, and rock 'n' roll. It's a realistic picture of one facet of the new China—but one that did not at all please the authorities. "I don't feel I make films attacking the political system. I draw pictures with my camera of daily life in cities, without exaggerating. Chinese society has some very violent sides. There's no shame in saying it or showing it."

A pariah in his own country, Zhang Yuan was nevertheless allowed to travel the world to promote his films—until March 1997. At that time the police, acting on orders from above, confiscated his passport to prevent him from presenting his *East Palace, West Palace*, a film that deals with homosexuality, at the Cannes Film Festival. Zhang had to submit to self-criticism sessions before being allowed to leave his country again in June 1998. "I'm lucky to be able to travel and make money, but I would prefer being able to work freely in my own country," he says. Zhang lives comfortably, although his savings are a pittance compared with the fortunes amassed by major movie stars and singers who have plunged headlong into a sea of green bills. Most performers, however, don't make that kind of money.

CLASS CULTURE

In the past, performing artists were members of state troupes. They could not express themselves freely, but they were paid enough to live on and had free housing. It was insalubrious housing, even for major performers such as the stars of the Central Ballet of China, who lived crammed together in studio apartments, but it was free. Today, performers still can't express themselves freely, and some of them aren't even paid anymore, owing to cutbacks throughout the public sector. Those who still receive their wages face a drop in their purchasing power because of inflation. Only big stars are doing well. With few exceptions, actors, musicians, and dancers have moved directly from a state of socialist semi-poverty to one of capitalist insecurity where the only art that counts is the art that sells. Socialism didn't lead to the development of a very high level of professionalism for most Chinese performers, with the exception of the circus. The market economy, without freedom of expression, seems to be nurturing co-optation and accommodation. As their stipends grow smaller and smaller, some small rural theater troupes have gone so far as to put on bawdy plays in order to survive, taking the risk of being banned from the stage for pornography!

The better-known theater companies have not reached that point. But they have felt the harsh effects of cutbacks, and they have been forced to downsize, the result being countless firings and early retirements. Plays are becoming more rare; it's hard to get everything together: Playwrights and directors spend most of their time racking their brains for ways to get around the censor, ways to live better. This has long been the case, of course, but the problem is now compounded by the necessity of making a profit. A play had better bring in money, because the state isn't there to cover debts.

In these lean times, performers have found one way to please everyone: They dig up old revolutionary shows. Choosing from among the eight operas and ballets authorized by Jiang Qing during the Cultural Revolution, they bring back classics like *The Girl with White Hair* and *Red Female Detachment*. Success at last! Young artists, who didn't live through the Red era when art had to provide political education to the masses, love performing these kitsch masterpieces. They play to packed houses of spectators who seem to be wondering whether to laugh or cry. In the end, the shows are seen as parodies of themselves. Audiences now pay good money to see plays that used to be put on for free back when the artist's noble mission was to awaken revolutionary consciousness. Socialist realism is incredibly entertaining, and people will even pay to see it—as long as it's not compulsory!

The government knows that these productions are just money-making schemes; nonetheless, it is delighted to see a popular success that harbors no dangers. Only the incorrigible Marxist dinosaurs of the Propaganda Department still believe in the instructional virtues of these shows. Intellectuals find the staging of these performances acceptable on a commercial level but troubling on an artistic one. According to them, these remakes, even with the dust shaken off them, are testament to the cultural desert that is spreading over the entire art world.

This cultural drought is deplored by one ex-professor from the Fine Arts Institute. He feels some responsibility for the situation: After years of hopeful struggle as a teacher, trying to awaken the creative spirit in his students, he gave up—partly in disgust and partly because a new career beckoned. He now works as a financial advisor in a bank. In addition to this generously remunerated position, he commissions copies of well-known paintings and sells them to hotels, restaurants, and other public places. A young artist can produce a copy in only one day. The professor pays 300 to 500 yuan per painting and then sells it for five times that price. This kind of work eases painters' financial worries and allows the professor to accumulate a nice little nest egg. One painter, exiled in Europe, comments: "Chinese artists have been too poor for too long. It's only fair that they should make a little money. You can't blame them even if most of them don't pay much attention to what they do."

In the last analysis, it seems clear that contemporary Chinese culture involves an immense waste of talent and money. The potential exists for a dynamic policy that would satisfy artists and the public as well. There's no doubt about it. But it hasn't materialized. The regime heralded its liberalization of the entertainment market as a means of raising the quality of productions, but everyone knows that the goal of the state was to save money. The main result has been an increase in ticket prices. By the mid-1990s, theater tickets cost from 50 to 100 yuan, peaking at 200 or even 300 for classical concerts with foreign orchestras in halls whose acoustics are almost good enough for Party congresses.

It's the same in publishing. The abrupt rise in the price of paper and the editors' need to secure funds from sources other than the state have brought about an extraordinary rise in the price of books. At the end of 1996, it was hard to find a new book for less than 20 yuan. Movies, too, are more expensive; tickets cost from 10 to 30 yuan, and the few really good films always cost the most. These prices are totally out of proportion to the purchasing power of the average person.

Culture in Deng's China is a way for the nouveaux riches to amuse themselves; it's not for the proletariat. From mass culture, China has turned to class culture. Tough luck for the poor.

Chapter *Nine*

THE CHINESE AND THE BARBARIANS

To a foreigner who asked why Chinese TV news always starts with national events, no matter what is happening elsewhere in the world, an amazed TV director responded quite seriously: "Why, because it's the *national* news, of course!" The director wasn't especially dim as far as Chinese bureaucrats go, but the question seemed ridiculous to him—incomprehensible. One can imagine him thinking: "Where else would we start? With foreign news? Do you think Chinese TV should start its prime-time news program talking about the outside world, the barbarians? Why, by Saint Mao? There's so much to say about our great and beautiful country." This is Beijing, the Chinese are speaking to the Chinese.

On with the "current events" of the Middle Kingdom—propaganda reports, some pathetic, others so fantastic as to be unintentionally funny. "Good thing for the ads" is Xiao Bai's wry comment. The only exceptions to this Sino-centrism are when China plays a leading role in an international event, political, economic, or sporting. Even then, attention is focused not on the event, but on China's role in it.

The government has increasingly emphasized nationalism since the beginning of the 1990s, as if to compensate for the crumbling of communism. Although Beijing officially refuses to admit the failure of Maoism (which would mean accepting responsibility and accountability to the people), the social and economic legacies of Mao are gradually being swept away. His goal, aside from his own maniacal personal ambition, was the construction of an egalitarian society. The goal that has gained ascendancy under Deng and his successors is the transformation of China into a great power. In the process, the people have lost their last shred of confidence in the cruel, corrupt Party; today, the people seem to believe only in money. The only social project that the government proposes to them is modernization, and the only ideology—the only glue to hold the people together—is nationalism.

The government is keeping alive a thousand-year-old xenophobic tradition that divides the world into two parts, center and periphery. Around the center—China, the Han nation—revolve the barbarians, the non-Chinese—"people of the outside" (*laowai*). Even when traveling abroad, Chinese people refer to others in this way, just as they would if they were in China.

To fan the flames of patriotic feeling, the government regularly blows on the coals of colonial humiliation, claiming that colonialism was responsible for China's slow economic development. This is partly true: Nineteenth-century colonialism severely damaged this country, which, a hundred years earlier, had won Western admiration for its high level of technical and commercial development and for its capacity to export wealth while preserving its own market. Official historians gloss over errors committed by the imperial dynasties, including their refusal to modernize out of fear of contaminating their civilization with "barbarian" ways at the time of the industrial revolution in the West.

This isolationism was carried forward by the Communist Party until Deng Xiaoping arrived in power. "Count on one's own strength," that was Mao's famous slogan, inspired by the desire to exalt the Han as well as to prove the superiority of socialism. Chinese leaders in the 1990s do not wish to make the same mistake. The development of a powerful country implies opening borders and playing a major role in world affairs. On the other hand—and here it gets tricky—xenophobic nationalism is one of the Chinese dictatorship's last mainstays. The more fragile the regime becomes (torn by internecine struggles, overwhelmed by social problems), the more it embraces the logic of difference and superiority and revives traditional racism.

The Communist Party must appear as the savior of the most brilliant civilization on the planet, a civilization that is supposedly under attack from all sides. You feel this catch-all patriotism everywhere, in school flag-raising events, sports events, speeches about Taiwan, and even in speeches about AIDS and drugs, which are denounced as plagues from the outside world. The government forgets to mention that the drug trade is run by Chinese organized crime, including the triads of the mainland.

The authorities' occasional patriotic campaigns are the object of ridicule by the Chinese people. For example, in 1996 the government went to war against words left over from the colonial era, suppressing foreign names for Chinese products and for public places such as restaurants and bars. Shopkeepers are well aware that a product with an English name sells better—even if it's only an imitation. Salespeople are torn between their pride at belonging to a great country and their endless fascination with developed countries. (Those of the West, that is. Japan, the Land of the Rising Sun, is remembered primarily for the suffering inflicted on China in the 1930s.) Fighting linguistic imperialism from the past is a losing battle, but the government doesn't seem to care. The regime's motivation may be simply to maintain feelings of difference, to provoke feelings of resentment—feelings that might lead to the desire for revenge. Either way it's a cynical calculation.

Lesson One: Foreigners are richer than Chinese people. Although this is no longer as true as it once was, "long noses" are still expected to pay when they come to China. Until 1995, China had special coins and bills reserved for foreigners; they've since been eliminated for economic reasons, but the idea remains current that "people from outside" should be charged more than natives. The state unhesitatingly applies a double standard in the fees it charges for transportation, hotels, tourist attractions, and lodging. Entrance to a public museum can cost up to ten times more for a foreigner as compared with a Chinese person. This organized racket has two advantages: It's wildly profitable, and it cultivates the idea of difference between peoples. It is only natural that the people go on to apply the concept. Even toilet attendants sometimes double their prices for outsiders. The foreigner, furious at having paid twice as much as a Chinese friend to relieve himself, may ask the following stupid question: "Why don't I pay the same as she does?" to which the toilet lady will respond as ingenuously as did the TV director: "But you are a foreign guest!"

Lesson Two: The Han civilization is superior to all others; a great destiny awaits China, but it could be thwarted by evil foreigners. To prove this, the government has launched a massive campaign of information—and disinformation. It's easy for the authorities to get their message across when the people are themselves justifiably proud of their past, and when the press is entirely submissive.

The Chinese civilization is one of the most ancient in the world, but it is not responsible for every single discovery on the planet. Nevertheless, the government has taken on the Herculean task of proving just that. Some Chinese people know that this is nonsense, but they condone maintaining the illusion, for propaganda purposes. Others believe the assertions that are made, with or without evidence.

It's known throughout the world that the Chinese invented gunpowder, the wheelbarrow, and the cultivation of silkworms. But did they really invent golf? the fork? public toilets? fast food? China claims all these inventions. Besides the media, which shamelessly trots out these assertions, there's specialized literature on the subject. The Chinese *Book of Records,* two hundred pages long, lists with imperial aplomb a multitude of "firsts" and "greatests." In the "Science" chapter, one can read that China is the first country in the world to use the "anti-hail." Wow! How do you prove that? Through a work of the Qing dynasty, in the seventeenth century, reporting the use of a "hail cannon" in Gansu province. China is also apparently the first country in the world to have proved, two thousand years ago, that light travels in a straight line. China is the first country to have understood the "notion of the limit" (though the excesses of its long history might lead one to doubt this). Allegedly China is also the inventor of the chromatic scale; it is the first country in the world to have noted the fall of meteorites; and it has the most salt lakes. Humanity would still be in the Stone Age were it not for the Han civilization. China even goes so far as to brag about possessing the river that floods the most often (the Yellow River) and the first case of syphilis (recorded well before Mao caught the illness). Records that other countries might hide away in embarrassment, the Chinese put forward as proof of their legendary superiority.

WHITE IS BEAUTIFUL

China's tenacious superiority complex coexists with a growing adoration of the West. The Chinese realize perfectly well that the advances of their once-brilliant civilization have fallen behind those of Europe and America. One segment of the Chinese population follows the official line and blames the lag on the foreigners who colonized and then pillaged the country after the Opium Wars of the nineteenth century. More and more people, however, realize that the imperial and Communist dynasties are the main culprits.

The policy of openness and the rise in purchasing power have made it possible for the Chinese people to sample Western goods. The Chinese may be xenophobic, but they're also pragmatic; they try to copy the "long noses." This practice extends to imitating holidays and traditions such as Valentine's Day and Santa Claus. Of course, these fads have taken hold only in big cities, and the commercial motivation is obvious. Nonetheless, in appropriating Western ways, the Chinese show their desire to join the world—in their own way.

Women are very important in this regard. Proud of their bodies and their skin, which they feel loses its beauty more slowly than does the skin of Western women, Chinese women are somewhat frustrated, because the world's canon of beauty is on the other side of the Great Wall. WHITE IS BEAUTIFUL—that seems to be the slogan. In the 1980s, Chinese women fixed their eyes and noses; now they dye their hair red or brown. They have their breasts surgically enlarged to imitate the "real breasts" seen in magazines and foreign films. For those who choose not to go under the scalpel, there are new bras that accentuate the best in the bust, while adding a little cotton padding just in case. Bottoms "as flat as the steppes of Mongolia"—says Xiao Bai—plunge Chinese women into profound despair, although Western women are seen as a bit too voluptuous. Something in between would be nice. For that, there are panty-girdles.

When it comes to fashion and beauty, the Chinese swear by France. For the rest, America is a fascinating annoyance. How could such a young country have succeeded so quickly, running the world with its money and its army? This question really gets to the Chinese, who join wholeheartedly with their leaders in denouncing American imperialism and accusing the United States of preaching lessons and policing the world—even as the Chinese consume the fruits of this empire with evident pleasure.

America is everywhere in China. It's not only a matter of Coca-Cola, McDonald's, Boeing, pop music, and basketball; it's also evident in mind-sets and behaviors. Copying Uncle Sam, the Chinese glorify individualism and personal success. In private, some leaders even praise the American dream without reservation. They preach American-style free enterprise and economic liberalism, vaunting even the Western nation's inequalities; they claim frankly that China should set out on the same road—which, in fact, the country comes closer to doing every day. This doesn't prevent the same people from affirming, in official meetings, their belief in the meaningless concept of "socialism with Chinese characteristics."

"Where would any Chinese person like to live, besides China?" asks Zhang Donghua. "In America, of course. What did the young demonstrators in Tiananmen Square do? They built a 'Goddess of Democracy' that looked like the Statue of Liberty. What did the Chinese Basketball Federation do to promote this very popular sport? They created a professional championship on the model of the NBA, going so far as to give their teams names resembling those of American teams. I call that fascination, don't you?" One could also cite the Chinese people's reaction to Bill Clinton's 1992 election. They were seized with admiration that the head of the most powerful country in the world, who was democratically elected, was only forty-six years old, while the destiny of their great country rested in the trembling hands of half-senile octogenarians and their doddering heirs apparent, themselves well advanced in age.

The government—which, secretly, is just as impressed by everything made in the USA—allows all of this to go on, aware that admiration can easily turn to rivalry and nurturing the private hope that there will be two superpowers in the next century: the Middle Kingdom and the United States. Two giants, full of respect and admiration for each other. If certain features distinguish the two nations one from the other—the length of their histories, for example—the two nations have other traits in common, such as the size of their territories, nationalism, and megalomania. In China as in America, everything has to be big, bigger, the biggest, colossal, more colossal. Terrifyingly large buildings, gargantuan servings of food, thundering laughter.

The Chinese and the Americans, ambitious political rivals, understand each other better than one might guess based on the crises that regularly erupt between Beijing and Washington. These protracted showdowns, full of suspense, always conclude with the happy ending secretly desired on both sides of the Pacific—even though the issues may be real ones, such as the question of Taiwan.

The crisis of February-March 1996 between the nationalist island, with its democratically elected president, and the mainland Communist regime gave the two giants a chance to test each other in the military domain, both knowing that they would not go so far as to confront each other. China was able to judge its own capacity to mobilize its population over an issue touching on "the unity of the country" and the "sovereignty of the nation" (this was the official jargon used every day in the Chinese newspapers during those two months). The government's first goal was to reaffirm loud and clear that Taiwan was "an inalienable part of China" which would be returned to the continental fold, by force if necessary. There would be no independence. Beijing's secondary goal was to harass President Lee Teng-Hui as he tried to get down to business after Taiwan's first presidential primary that applied universal suffrage—a democratic system of nomination Chinese leaders reject in the name of the famous Chinese "exception." Taiwan's democratic elections created a new, delicate propaganda problem for Beijing: how to claim that Taiwan was one hundred percent Chinese while arguing that Taiwan's democracy would never work in China.

The first goal was achieved thanks to an impressive deployment of force in the straits of Taiwan, including missile firings immediately next to the Taiwanese coast. But China was unable to prevent the incumbent president from winning reelection. There was no independent opinion poll to measure the impact of this election on the Chinese. But it seems clear that there is a difference of opinion, maybe even a rupture, between the people and the government. Ask a Chinese person if Taiwan belongs to China, and he'll say yes. Ask him if he's ready to fight to recover the island, to fulfill his "sacred mission" as defined by the regime, and he'll say no.

COMPATRIOTS

Zhang Donghua has relatives in Taiwan—an elderly aunt on his father's side who fled China before 1949 with her husband, a civil servant in the nationalist ranks. In 1983 Zhang met his aunt for the first time. At the time, he was still spinning his wheels at the post office. He remembers this historic visit as if it were yesterday. With hindsight, he thinks that his aunt's first visit to the mainland in thirty-five years profoundly influenced his decision to give up the "iron rice bowl." He remembers how antsy his father was the night before their visitor arrived. The Zhang family had spent countless hours cleaning and rearranging their little two-room apartment. There was no question of having the prestigious guest stay in a hotel, although she was on a guided tour and the Zhang residence was hardly spacious. Donghua would go sleep with a neighbor (all of the neighbors knew what was going on).

Zhang heard all kinds of advice. "In Taiwan, they have this. In Taiwan, they have that. Better buy some or she'll be uncomfortable. In Taiwan, it's like this, it's like that...." The father was afraid of losing face before his sister. He panicked, to the total exasperation of his wife, who had been slaving away for weeks to provide her sister-in-law with an impeccable welcome. Mr. Zhang the communist knew that his compatriots in Taiwan—the civil war's losers, the runaways—had a higher standard of living. Their lifestyle was more modern, more Western. He was trying to do damage control, to show that there was some good in socialism, that maybe it was even better in some ways.

As might be expected, the reunion was punctuated with endless tearful scenes. But what impressed Zhang Donghua were not the sad moments, but his aunt's evocations of daily life on the island: young people's aspirations and the chance for the bold and brave to make money. He could tell that she found Mainland China backward and suffocating, despite the fact that she herself was "a traditional Chinese woman." China was changing quickly, but the woman from Taiwan had little basis for comparison other than a few dim memories of life before 1949.

Zhang Donghua remembers the night when his aunt invited the whole family to a restaurant in a brand-new four-star hotel, a manifestation of the intention of Mao's successors to open the country to Western capital. The enormous buffet offered both Western and Chinese dishes. Zhang Donghua choose only foreign food, purposely selecting dishes whose names and composition were unknown to him. He was already showing signs of individuality; most Chinese people take few chances on Western dishes. He devoured a huge ice-cream special, with four scoops covered in whipped cream. It was the most ice cream he had ever eaten in his life. His parents seemed embarrassed, off balance in this luxurious place, and they barely managed to eat despite constant encouragement from the aunt. Only the young man relished this moment of happiness, a new, simple happiness. When it came time for the check, Mr. Zhang and his wife couldn't help blanching, while trying to keep up appearances so as not to ruin the evening. The bill was 500 yuan, ten times their monthly earnings! The price of this unforgettable meal later became a subject of contention between Mr. and Mrs. Zhang. "She flaunted her wealth to humiliate us" was the refrain of the postal clerk's mother. Zhang Donghua took no interest in this clash, he could care less about the bill. What captivated him was the method of payment: the credit card.

The aunt never returned to China; apparently, seeing the land of her ancestors one last time was enough for her. The families keep up a regular correspondence, waiting for the day when people from the mainland will be able to visit the island freely. If for that reason only, the Zhang family wishes for peaceful reunification—or else a peaceful separation, if a split is unavoidable. In any case, it's a "Chinese matter"; the issue of the future of Taiwan should be resolved among the Chinese. That's why the citizens of the People's Republic of China disapproved of the presence of an American armada around Taiwan at the time of the 1996 elections—a sentiment shared even by those most critical of the ruling regime. "Let them mind their own business" was the attitude, the underlying understanding being that the future of Taiwan is purely a Chinese question just as was the future of Hong Kong.

It is an understatement to say that the reversion of the British colony to China came at a convenient time for a worn-out regime that, having once brandished nationalism as a weapon, now leans on it as a crutch. The recovery of territories stolen by the British has allowed China to harp on misfortunes endured during and after the two opium wars in the nineteenth century. The "taking"—or rather "retaking"—of Hong Kong by Beijing on July 1, 1997, signified the absorption by the last great Communist dinosaur of one of the most beautiful jewels of world capitalism. And, for Chinese leaders, taking back Hong Kong was also an act of revenge against the West. The dismantling of democratic institutions in the Special Administrative Region of Hong Kong is designed not only to ensure that no Chinese region will be governed by universal suffrage, but also to show that Beijing is in charge—that London is out of the picture.

At the end of 1996, after a travesty of elections, Beijing named the future chief executive of the postcolonial era: Tung Chee-hwa, a wealthy shipowner from Shanghai. This patriot and his government are in thrall to the Communist Party politburo. No concession was made to the people of Hong Kong or to the British, who called for a democratically elected local assembly similar to the one formed in the colony in 1995. China, jubilant and malicious, retorted that since it took the British a century to set up any Western-style democracy in Hong Kong, the former colonizers can hardly complain.

China has promised to maintain for at least fifty years the economic system that allowed Hong Kong to become a major force in world finance and investment. The Chinese are applying a policy of "one country, two systems." So as not to kill off the goose that lays the golden eggs, China is leaning on Chinese billionaires in Hong Kong, tycoons like Tung Chee-hwa, who, willingly or not, have chosen to declare themselves "patriots." The Chinese government's reassurance about respecting Hong Kong's freedom in economic matters has not been enough to prevent the exodus of some of Hong Kong's 6 million people. The majority of the island's population are refugees and the children of refugees who fled the Communist regime; since 1989, thousands have fled to the United States, Australia, and Canada.

China did not return to Hong Kong with a knife in its teeth as some had feared. The Chinese didn't want to frighten the people, or the investors, or the Taiwanese. In recovering Hong Kong, Beijing wanted to demonstrate that it could also reunify peaceably with the nationalist island—that China is not an ogre.

An ogre? Maybe not. But will Taiwan and Hong Kong sate Deng's successors? The authorities have a nasty habit of finding ever more "Chinese matters"—matters that involve extending the country's borders. The most insistent claim is for the disputed archipelagos in the South China Sea. An impressive increase in Chinese military presence there has worried other countries in the region. China's territorial claims for one or another of these atolls have about the same degree of historical basis as the inventions in the book of records. "A lie told one hundred times becomes true," says a Chinese proverb—and some part of the immense population of China may well end up believing these irredentist claims.

But Beijing has to be careful that whipping up nationalist feeling doesn't backfire. In late 1996, the Chinese government banned anti-Japanese demonstrations provoked by the matter of the Diaoyu Islands, which have been claimed by China, Japan, and Taiwan. Although the demonstrations were in line with government policy, the regime was frightened that they might turn into anticommunist gatherings.

With expansionist ambitions, China kills two birds with one stone: It causes anxiety to the international community, especially the United States, China's rival in the Far East and Southeast Asia, and at the same time it bolsters public confidence in China's ability to play a major role on the world scene.

Pressing and potentially violent national questions also exist within China's borders, particularly at the far reaches of the empire, in the so-called "minority" regions of Xinjiang and Tibet and, to a lesser extent, Inner Mongolia. Prior to the establishment of the People's Republic, Chinese Communists had planned that these regions would be independent members of a federation of republics. But once the Communists came to power, Mao vigorously opposed the separation of Han China from the fifty or so "national minorities" who now make up 10 percent of the total population but occupy 60 percent of the national territory. Mao's word being law, the concept of self-determination was buried after 1949 and replaced by the concept of national unity, which is supposedly necessary in the interests of resisting foreign aggression. This is still the official line. But tensions are mounting dangerously, and the Chinese government has been having trouble keeping order in these regions. Particularly turbulent are places where the Han are in a minority, such as Xinjiang, a vast region encompassing over one-sixth the total area of China, situated along the borders of Central Asia.

"In your country, it's easy to get arms? Here, it's hard. We could use them, though." This snatch of a conversation in the middle of the night between a foreigner and a young Uïgur after an accidental meeting on the streets of Korla, in the center of the region, says much about the tension that exists in what used to be eastern Turkestan. Arms, to do what? "To throw the Chinese out," responds Youssef without hesitation, like the hardened warrior that he is not yet but may be one day. For the moment, Youssef is just a student at Urumqi University, with an adolescent face lit up by large, sparkling green eyes. An unruly lock of auburn hair sweeps across his large forehead. Physically, Youssef doesn't look like a Han, any more than do the other "national minorities" of the region. He is Uïgur, Turkic-speaking, and proud of it. He is not politically active but it wouldn't take much to persuade him to join one of the clandestine movements that cause so many problems for the Beijing regime. At least that's what he seemed to want to communicate to his interviewer. His Mandarin is halting but comes stuttering out with machine-gun intensity. His family lives in a little ground floor cobwall house without comfort, decorated with shimmering oriental tapestries, flaking paintings of Mecca, and a calendar illustrated with pictures of veiled dancers—all of this covered by a film of dust thick enough to remind one that Korla is the last great northern oasis before the implacable sands of the Taklamakan Desert. The decorations don't hide the disintegration of the walls. There are two light brown Formica chests of drawers, one in the living room and one in the room that serves as a bedroom to the student and his father and brother-in-law. Of the bric-a-brac arranged there, not one trinket is Chinese. In Youssef's home, there are no Buddha-shaped piggy banks or miniature models of the buried soldiers of Xian.

Whether sitting on the leatherette sofa in Youssef's living room or wandering through the dirt alleyways of his neighborhood, the visitor has trouble convincing himself that he is in China. A heavy colonial perfume floats in the air, mixing with the stench of the bloody slaughtered sheep hanging in doorways. Haunting music evokes an imaginary country located somewhere between Arabia and Persia. There's no trace of China, no trace of the Chinese—except in the Han neighborhood, which looks like it could be in any eastern city, with its brick and parpen buildings, its grocery stores, its school. The Han cluster together, keeping to themselves, eating Chinese food, speaking Chinese. "The officials sent here don't have to learn our language while we, we have to know Chinese," Youssef says. "They even tried to suppress the teaching of the Uïgur language a few years ago, but the resistance was too strong. The most intelligent Chinese have understood that they must make concessions if they want to stay in our country as long as possible."

The segregation between Han and non-Han exists in all of the cities of the Xinjiang region, whether the Chinese are a minority or a majority. In Xinjiang, they officially make up a bit more than a third of the population and the Uïgurs 47 percent, the rest being ethnic Kazakhs or Tadjiks. But in Urumqi, the capital and the administrative and political center, it's the other way around. The city is becoming more and more Chinese. Minarets are disappearing behind office buildings, shopping centers, and karaokes, all covered with ideograms. Merchants from the provinces in the center of the country are flocking in to make their fortunes along the ancient Silk Road. They're supported and encouraged by their local leaders, who are only too happy to find a partial solution to the unemployment problem. In Beijing, the central government is secretly glad about this new form of colonization.

Political leaders in Xinjiang, whether Chinese or members of a "national minority," claim publicly that ethnic groups in the region live "in harmony." But they know very well that this is not true. Different groups do work side by side in the public sector, but elsewhere, Chinese and non-Chinese don't usually occupy the same posts, and when they do, they don't become friendly. They ignore each other as much as possible. A little educational game for visitors to Xinjiang: Watch a city street for an hour and count the number of times you see Chinese people and Uïgurs walking together. There's not much friendship, and even less love. Inter-ethnic marriages don't happen. They'd be considered treasonous—on both sides.

Politically, many non-Chinese ally themselves with the Communist Party, but not out of a commitment to communism or to China; it's a matter of security, the comfort of a quiet little life as an official. At the same time, the non-Chinese may hedge their bets. In Xinjiang, many Party members sympathize with the cause of independence and some are secretly active. In many places, separatists permeate the Communist Party. The authorities of the central government are continually threatening severe punishment for officials who tolerate or sympathize with secessionists.

The political climate in what used to be called Eastern Turkestan, known as Xinjiang since its annexation by the People's Republic of

China, started to heat up after the Soviet Union fragmented in 1991. Emerging from that breakup were Central Asian republics populated in part by the same ethnic groups that live in Xinjiang. It wasn't hard for independence groups to set up their headquarters on the other side of the ex-Sino-Soviet border, which became a sieve for men and arms. In May 1996 China signed a border-zone security agreement with the three neighboring Central Asian republics, hoping that improved regional military cooperation would strengthen China's hand. The separatist movement was gaining momentum at that time, according to Kazakhstan-based activists who kept track of the number of attacks and demonstrations. The official press in the region increased the virulence of its anti-separatist rhetoric at the beginning of 1996, revealing growing anxiety. There was also an attack, in broad daylight on an Urumqi street, on an official of Uïgur origin, the vice president of the regional consultative council of the Chinese people. Was this a feud between Uïgurs, or was it provocation by Chinese security forces? Several imams, accused by the extremists of cooperating with Chinese authorities, were reportedly beaten, according to unconfirmed accounts. Other imams, too openly engaged in the separatist movement, were stripped of their religious posts by the Communist Party, which has the power to name or depose clergy of all faiths throughout the country.

Xinjiang religious leaders are defiant toward those whom most of the faithful consider to be invaders. But they remain less politically involved than the Tibetan monks, who have spearheaded the protest movement in the Roof of the World.

Since 1951, when the Chinese army entered Tibet to "liberate the region peaceably," active resistance has been led by the Buddhist clergy. The Dalaï Lama, spiritual leader of the Tibetans, exiled since the failed anti-Chinese uprising in 1959, is also their main political leader. When he received the Nobel Peace Prize in 1989, the prestige he gained allowed the "living God" to travel throughout the world and be received with honors almost everywhere. The Chinese government, scandalized, was quick to denounce the awarding of the prize as foreign interference in China's internal affairs. The Nobel Prize gave hope to the Tibetans at a time when the anti-Chinese movement in Tibet was getting its second wind. The Chinese regime had misjudged the religious fervor that animates the Kingdom of Snow. After the extremes of the Cultural Revolution, Beijing reformers concluded that the power of religion in Tibet would dwindle as the economy progressed. Instead, a softening in Chinese policies on religious matters opened the way for a resurgence of the resistance movement in 1987.

Tibetan Buddhism is the foundation of Tibetan civilization, holding it together and also serving as a weapon, playing a much more important role than does Islam in Xinjiang. Beijing will have difficulty getting out of the Tibetan quagmire, but there is one small advantage compared to the Xinjiang problem: There's only one people, not an ethnic mosaic. The fight is targeted, even if there are disagreements among Tibetan groups in exile about the strategy to adopt against the occupier. These disagreements are exploited politically by the Communist regime and sometimes aggravated by secret agents who infiltrate Tibetan organizations.

So far, all the various tactics adopted by China to resolve the Tibetan question have failed. Violence has been the worst failure of all. Arrests, imprisonment, and torture have not defused the separatist tendencies of the Tibetans. Vexed, Beijing criticizes those, in Tibet or elsewhere, who denounce human rights violations in the region but never mention the cruelty of the Tibetan feudal system before "liberation." In 1996 both the Chinese government and the Dalaï Lama set out to choose the child who would be the reincarnation of the Panchen Lama, the second in the Tibetan hierarchy. The previous Panchen Lama had died in 1989. The Tibetans rejected the Chinese choice, and there was a new upsurge of violence.

In objecting to the Nobel Peace Prize, the Chinese government once again made clear to the Tibetans, to the Chinese, and to the international community that China intends to remain master of the Roof of the World. For Beijing, the matter is settled: Tibet has been attached to the Chinese empire since the thirteenth century, under the Yuan dynasty. There will be no independence. The government is ready to pay the price and invests massively in the region, hoping that economic colonization will discourage local people from pursuing the cause of independence.

The idea is to maintain the empire with bills rather than billy clubs. To have a chance of working, this policy must be accompanied by massive resettlement of Han people to the Tibetan region. The battle of numbers is ferocious between the Chinese and the Tibetans; the Tibetans accuse the Chinese of sending so many Han to Tibet that they will marginalize the Tibetans and finally annihilate their culture all together. Many outside observers agree that the imposition of Chinese culture in Tibet is a real phenomenon. Beijing sends not only soldiers but thousands of merchants, investors, and adventurers. Lhassa, the regional capital, is slowly being transformed into a modern Chinese city, surrounded by military garrisons.

In Xinjiang, black gold provides China with an additional motivation to invest its money and people. Geological studies have not yet shown the existence of any vast reserves, but the substrata contain abundant layers, and oil prospecting is proceeding. Beijing cleverly uses foreign oil companies to reinforce its control of the region. "Oil prospecting makes money for the Chinese, not for us. They keep the best jobs for themselves," affirms Youssef. The young rebel is right. The Han work the oil fields, and prospecting is designed primarily to benefit the eastern provinces, where the economic upswing has created a huge demand for energy. But the Chinese claim that the Uïgurs and other minorities—who have traditionally been merchants and herders—refuse to drill for oil in the desert. The work is too hard.

"That's true, I wouldn't spend my life in a sandy hell," admits Youssef, who also reproaches the Chinese for using his "country" to test nuclear bombs. "They pillage our oil and shower us with radioactivity," he complains. The site of Lop Nor, in Xinjiang, has been used for all of China's nuclear experiments since the explosion of the nation's first atomic bomb in 1964. "And what are we getting out of it?" asks the young man. He does admit that in the cities of his region, the standard of living for the average person has risen noticeably since 1990, and that the Chinese are not the only ones to take advantage of it. Far from it. Some Uïgurs have gotten rich, and some are millionaires.

Youssef also admits that he is allowed to study at the university, and that there is no systematic discrimination against minorities, as extremists sometimes claim. But it's not a good idea to dwell for too long on the theme that "the Chinese don't only do bad things." This bothers him, and finally he blows up: "It's our country. It's up to us to decide what's good and what's bad for us. It's not up to the Chinese or any other foreigner. For the moment, the Han tell us what to do. The Uïgurs in the regional government don't have any real power. At best, they can influence unimportant decisions." And he concludes menacingly, "If this goes on, we'll have to look for solutions elsewhere."

If young Uïgurs let themselves be seduced by political and religious extremism, the government has reason to worry. Judging by the rise in the number of violent attacks, the anti-Chinese movement is getting organized and radicalized. According to the National United Revolutionary Front (NURF), based in Kazakhstan, almost 60,000 Uïgurs were arrested in 1996. Of this number, 1,700 were executed, including a good number of mullahs and religious students from Koran schools.

In Xinjiang, as in Tibet, China risks locking itself into an inextricable situation. But it doesn't want to cede an inch of territory, for fear of encouraging separatist claims elsewhere. In Mongolia maybe, or why not Canton? The anxiety with which the Chinese approach "minority" issues can be seen in their embarrassment when discussing the traces of a small Jewish community in China, now reduced to a few thousand completely assimilated descendents of Jews. China likes national minorities only when they are performing folkloric dances for foreign tourists or for Party officials on inspection tours.

Like the huge majority of their countrymen, Professor Yao, Xiao Bai, and Sun Lin have never set foot in Xinjiang or in Tibet. All they know are the banalities transmitted by the official press or by friends who went there without trying to understand this "other China." Common clichés: "Tibetans are dirty," "It's hard to breathe at 4,000 meters of altitude," and "The Uïgurs are lazy but very hospitable." Zhang Donghua went to Xinjiang on business. His company has clothes made there out of cashmere, one of the region's main revenue sources besides oil. "It's on the old Silk Road. The Uïgurs have just as much commercial sense as the Chinese. We understand each other, and relations are amicable. Among all of the Uïgurs and Kazakhs that I know, no one openly argues for independence for Xinjiang. They're fine as long as they can do their business, but it's true that the crumbling of the USSR reawakened their nationalist sentiment. Among the more radical, there are hopes of freedom from Han tutelage," says the businessman. "You know, if the relations between the Han and the minorities are tense, there are also tensions between the ethnic groups themselves. You shouldn't reduce the question of Xinjiang to an opposition between Han and others. The situation is more complex. Some talk about a powder keg that hasn't exploded yet," adds Zhang, before getting down to brass tacks: "You want to know the only thing that really bothers me out there? The smell of mutton..."

The Chinese people don't seem overly concerned by the controversies over Tibet and Xinjiang. Unmoved by heavy-handed propaganda about the "duty" of an entire people to protect their country's sovereignty, they know that the Tibetans and the Uïgurs are different, that they're not Han and never will be. If these two distant regions want their independence, why stop them? How would this separation change the lives of Chinese people in the East? Han chauvinism among the people doesn't have the bellicose character promoted by official discourse.

Chinese dissidents tend to think more about the political future of their country than most Chinese. But for a long time they ignored the problem of the minorities, including Tibet and Xinjiang. Dissidents focused their efforts on the struggle for democracy and the rights of man—implicitly, for the Chinese man. Wei Jingsheng was one of the few exceptions. He approached this thorny problem during his first stint in prison. He wrote down some of his reflections, taking Deng Xiaoping to task concerning the Tibetan people's right to self-determination. These writings were later used as evidence against him at his second "trial," to show that he intended to overthrow the government!

Certain political activists who were forced into exile after 1989 have begun to take on the question of Tibet. Once abroad, they gained access to more information; they met with Tibetans, exiled like themselves, and they followed the activities of the Dalaï Lama, whose Nobel Prize was given in the year of the Tiananmen Square massacres. At long last, the publications of dissident groups in exile began to denounce human rights violations in Tibet and Xinjiang. Reflection about these lands continues. Debates, which take place in the West and especially in the United States where there is a significant pro-Tibetan lobby, furnish a good excuse for Beijing to denounce once again the interference of foreign countries in its internal affairs and the leading role of the Americans in this "venture of destabilization."

THE UNAVOIDABLE FOREIGNER

The Chinese government jumps at every chance to stigmatize the United States as nothing but a "paper tiger." At the same time, China needs American capital to develop its economy. The government cleverly manipulates commercial competition between Europeans and Americans, who squabble like dogs over a bone for the appetizing Chinese market. Any political difference between China and one of its trading partners leads to economic blackmail: "Don't criticize us

about human rights or we'll sign a contract with another country."
This tactic works, and China continues to absorb foreign capital from
around the world. This "cooperation" also means that Chinese people
spend more time with Westerners and are beginning to understand
more about how things work elsewhere in the world—outside the center. Chinese leaders try to maintain a delicate balance; they can't stop
the policy of economic opening—that would be suicidal—but they
don't want Western ideas to "pollute" the spirit of the people. As good
at sleight-of-hand as they are at balancing acts, the rulers manage to
attribute economic success to the Communist Party, to the greatness
of Chinese civilization, and to the intelligence of the people—not to
the foreigners.

Yet, what are the real reasons for China's economic miracle? Deng
didn't just wave a magic wand. It's true that he had the flair to understand that his country could finally move forward economically if it
broke out of its legendary isolation. He was right. Give Deng his due.
But in the last analysis, what made possible the rise in the standard of
living? Foreign investment. What allows Chinese people to live more
comfortably? Foreign goods. How are the Chinese informed? By the
foreign press. Which factories function well and make quality products? Joint ventures. Let's face it: The things that work really well in the
country do not belong exclusively to the Chinese. This is a bitter pill
for a proud people to swallow. The government pretends it's not true.
No one is fooled, but appearances are saved.

And another thing: Which Chinese people are the best trained?
Those who have studied abroad. Unfortunately for China, three
quarters of the young people who go to Western universities don't
return home once they graduate, even though there are employment
opportunities awaiting them at home. This brain drain saps a country that needs all the help it can get to carry out its ambitious
economic development. The situation is aggravated by the growing
number of teachers who are quitting to join the heady world of
business.

The Chinese government is trying hard to stop this hemorrhaging. The material conditions of life for returning graduates are improving. But this hasn't been enough. The powerful and deep sentiment of belonging to the Chinese nation—a sentiment that resists the erosion of time—does not arouse in expatriates the desire to work for their country. Individual interests take precedence over the general interest. Wielding the carrot and the stick, the authorities force those traveling abroad to leave behind an exorbitant security deposit (50,000 yuan in 1996) which they will never see again if they don't return. Even this measure, which hits people straight in the pocketbook, is not enough to persuade the expatriates to come back and "work for the construction of the country." The government should have understood long ago that you can't put a price on freedom. Maybe they do understand it but just don't want to admit it.

Countless young Chinese study abroad with the sincere intention of returning and then change their minds. Why this irresistible attraction for the West? It's not only the desire for better material circumstances; it's also the desire for freedom that leads many young Chinese people to seek out the West—and sometimes, to seek out a Western spouse. That was one of the motivations of Professor Yao's son when he decided to marry an American.

A LITTLE HELLO

For at least twenty minutes, Grampa Yao had been ensconced in the bathroom. Several times a day, the old man locked himself into his private hideaway with a daily paper or else with one of the old American magazines he kept carefully stashed away. Not even the Red Guard had found them when they ransacked his house in 1967. Grampa Yao liked to browse through his English-language collection, which he bought when he was working as an overseer at an American factory in Shanghai. That was before 1949, before the Communists chased out the foreign capitalist devils in the name of national sovereignty. Now, decades later, those same Communists called back the same foreign capitalists, in the name of progress.

A magazine in his hand, Grampa Yao fell into a reverie. He was still angry at the Communists for having deprived him of his livelihood and at the Americans for having abandoned him. Now in his eighties, he didn't know which he felt more strongly: his anticommunism or his anti-Americanism. While he brooded, his daughter Yao Minhua was losing patience waiting for her father to come out of the bathroom. Not that it was unusual for the old fellow to spend twenty minutes there. But she had something important to announce to him and was not sure how to soften the blow. It was about her nephew, Professor Yao's son. The young man was going to marry an American. The plan was not new, but no one had yet cleared it with the patriarch. Professor Yao hadn't had the nerve to call his father on the phone to announce the news; he had sent a letter, leaving it up to his sister to handle the delivery.

Grampa was dragging out his pleasurable moments of privacy, rereading an article about D-Day. Unable to stand it any longer, his daughter called out in a trembling voice through the door: "There's a letter from Yao Guoguang. Yao Ding is getting married." She had to repeat the news twice because her father had "forgotten" to put in his hearing aid. When he finally got the message he burst forth like a hurricane, although he usually carried his 220 pounds with the dignity of an elderly elephant. Falling into a chair, Grampa Yao insisted that his daughter read him the letter.

"Who's he going to marry?" he suddenly cried out.

"A businesswoman," responded Yao Minhua, whose forehead had started to bead with sweat. The old man noticed her discomfort.

"What is it, is she a Communist?" the old man asked sharply, raising himself up out of his seat with the help of his cane.

"Sit down, Papa, you'll feel better," his daughter said, preparing herself for the big moment.

"I'll sit down when you've told me what you have to tell me!" Grampa Yao snapped, annoyed.

"Papa, she's American." Yao Minhua didn't have time to rush to her father's side. He tottered and fell down in a faint.

When old Yao came to, he had forgotten what was going on.

"What happened?"

Before his daughter could come up with a lie to prevent the onset of another attack, one of the grandchildren cried out spontaneously, "It's Yao Ding. He's marrying an American," and the grandfather fainted again.

This story is famous in the Yao family, among all of the cousins and second cousins, too. It's been told and retold to dozens of friends and neighbors—who knows, it may even be circulating in the Chinatowns of Paris, New York, and Vancouver! It goes over well with several generations, especially since the grandfather ended up getting along with his American granddaughter-in-law (although he never stopped regretting that his grandson hadn't married a Chinese woman). Luckily, the American bride wasn't black. This would have been a bitter pill to swallow, for the Chinese don't like black people.

The long history of the Han people has not included any real contact with black people. The few Sino-African relations that exist today originate in Mao's policy of Third World economic cooperation in the face of "Yankee and Soviet imperialism." This policy, which involved generous technical and financial aid, served to extend China's influence in Africa. In 1995 a more pragmatic policy of interest-bearing loans was initiated (once more, economy prevails over ideology). Sino-African exchange programs allow a few thousand young Africans to study in China. But outside of diplomatic and university circles, Chinese people have little contact with blacks from Africa or from elsewhere in the world. Still, without ever having met a flesh-and-blood black person, they hate them. And they don't try to hide it.

"I don't like blacks." White foreigners are likely to hear this phrase, pronounced in disdainful tones, repeatedly. It's true that the color black is considered to bring bad luck. That doesn't make it any easier to understand the origin of this virulent racism which permeates society, touching even the most educated and open-minded. Maybe it's due to ignorance—in which case future contact should improve things. It depends, of course, on the kind of contacts.

Xiao Bai recounts an adventure she and one of her friends had a few years ago on the way home from school. Crammed into a bus jam-packed with passengers, the two were chattering away as usual when the bus stopped suddenly. Xiao Bai's friend was violently propelled a couple of yards; she grabbed firmly on to another passenger to keep from falling. When she raised her head to thank her savior, whose hand she was still holding, she got the shock of her life. The man was as black as ebony—a student no doubt, who had courageously strayed from campus to do a little shopping and get a sense of the real China. Well, he got it. Terrorized, the girl yanked back her hand and screamed. She had touched a black person for the first time in her life and she was as scared as if she were confronted with a snake! The other passengers all turned to look suspiciously at the African, wondering what he had done to the poor little Chinese girl.

Sun Lin admits without embarrassment that she stays on her guard. On the rare occasions when she runs across a black person in the street or in a store, she can't help being scared. When she was selling pirate CDs in the diplomatic neighborhoods, she never approached black passers-by but merely stared at them as if they were strange beasts. Why? "I don't know, I just can't stand them," she replies uncertainly, adding, "They're dirty." In response to the remark that many Chinese spit frequently, that their respect for the environment could be faulted, and that peasants don't exactly wash every single day, the cleaning lady responds, "It's not the same, I find them dirty because of the black."

Despite the veneration of the young for "the two Michaels" (Jordan and Jackson), young people are not immune to anti-black racism. Verbal jousting matches explode on campuses between Chinese and African students, usually over the rare girls who are willing to go out with African men. Chinese male students seem particularly incensed by the sight of female students going around with blacks. If any girl complains that she was bothered by an African, things can get violent. In 1989, just a few months before the beginning of the freedom movement, demonstrations broke out on Beijing campuses on this issue. The incidents that prompted the protest are unclear, but the students' slogan was HANDS OFF THE CHINESE WOMAN! Beijing students were soon to become the toast of the world for their courage and high ideals; they were to make the regime tremble. But on this subject the students demonstrated with the blessing of the authorities! On the question of national identity, the elite of the nation's youth were not any more "open" than the "closed-minded" old Communists. In fact, the concept of "the Chinese race" is widely accepted by opponents and defenders of the regime alike. It's a shared value, like the belief in the value of money. The Han use the term *race*, whose ideogram also means "minority."

The reactions that greet mixed couples illustrate perfectly the paradoxical sentiments emerging from a feeling of racial superiority combined with a fascination with the West. The professor's son and his American wife face constant kidding. They're always getting told off— but only in jest, since the man is Chinese and the woman foreign. Couples in the opposite situation face not jokes, but insults. Men— usually young men—make comments, often in slang to prevent the husband from understanding, and in low voices to avoid making a scene. "Look at her, traitor to the Chinese race, shame!" This is the remark best remembered by one of Yao Ding's friends. She heard this on the beach on the island of Hainan one summer night; the insult came from a man with the pompous bearing of a Beijing official. This same young woman, who is married to a Frenchman, remembers what happened when she told off a fellow who had blatantly shoved into the queue at a museum entrance.

"Wait in line like everyone else!" she snapped.

"Just because you're with a foreigner doesn't mean you can lord it over everyone else!" the man retorted.

The French husband remembers this phrase: "First he stole the flower, then the fruit." He was walking through the Beijing clothes market with a Chinese woman—not his wife, but a friend, who was five months pregnant—when this comment came at him from a young vendor. Older people never make such remarks, but their eyes seem to; and some whisper.

The rise in mixed marriages owing to the presence of more and more foreign residents shows that not all Chinese are repelled by *métissage*. Strangely, while Chinese people look askance at marriage with a Westerner, they admire Eurasian children immensely. They are persuaded that the offspring of these "treacherous" relationships are particularly intelligent, according to a dubious theory about the mixing of distant blood.

The professor wasn't surprised that his son decided to marry an American. For years Yao Ding had a little group of Chinese friends who loved to speak English and dreamt of leaving the country. They spent all their time with foreigners. Professor Yao knew that there was no point in trying to thwart his son's plans—the boy was stubborn by nature. In any case, the professor is one of those fatalistic intellectuals who lost what remained of their illusions during the Cultural Revolution and live in constant anticipation of another national catastrophe. He'd like to be able to protect his children against the next misfortune of this country, whatever it may be. With China's mad rush forward it is hard to know what will happen next. Professor Yao's convinced that his son is better off with an American passport—it'll be a shield, a flying carpet.

The only hesitation the professor has about his son's marriage is the risk of divorce. Many such joint ventures flounder. Cultural differences, as enriching as they may be, lead to too many misunderstandings. All the goodwill in the world may not be enough to surmount these difficulties. However, the professor reasoned, if the divorce rate of Westerners is high, it's rising in China, too. All in all, Yao Ding's marriage to the Californian had more advantages than disadvantages.

When Professor Yao heard that his daughter-in-law was pregnant, it did strike him that the child would not be 100 percent Han. "But he'll be named Yao," he thought. And he immediately began to adore the little Buffalo—the baby's sign according to Chinese astrology.

No one in the family doubts that the child will be a little Chinese-American god. Ning Ning is delighted—she's going to have a sort of little brother, born in the country of Mickey Mouse. "A Little Hello!" she nicknamed him, giggling.

Conclusion

January 1997. The Year of the Rat draws to a close.

Zhang Donghua travels through the United States with the firm intention to open a store with leather clothing or some other product. He has already met with several important and powerful representatives from the Chinese mafia in North America as well as Chinese diplomats in Washington, to assist him with his venture. He plans to bring his family to the United States or Canada and to register his son at an American secondary school for "spoiled rich kids."

Professor Yao himself will also travel to the United States to visit his first Chinese-American grandchild. He will then retire and receive 500 yuan each month. Fortunately, his parallel activities go well. Tired of following his diet, he recommenced with his habit of 4 liters of beer a day, absorbed by foods high in fat. His wife worries, not him. He is living again.

Sun Lin still works for Mrs. Chen and continues to save money. She is getting ready to return to her village with her husband to celebrate the lunar New Year and to above all see their child who almost died from improperly cared for meningitis. The little peasant from

Henan no longer goes to the cinema in Beijing, as she finds that there are not any good movies and that it is too expensive.

Xiao Bai seriously thinks about getting back her freedom, dreaming of not always being number two. The "concubine" is inclined to relinquish the material goods which were attributed to her and hopes to convince her unofficial husband to "set her free." She wants to take up her studies again in a private university or to embark into business. A friend advised her to open a chic bar in Beijing where she would profit from the "white-collar class."

Deng Xiaoping held on for another year, but rumors of a deterioration of his state of health circulated. Economic growth settled at 10 percent in 1996 versus a little more than 2 percent in both France and the U.S. Foreign investments reached 40 million dollars, 16 percent more than in 1995. The regime prepares for the return of Hong Kong to the motherland with great fanfare. The peasants do not cease from flocking to the cities. Wei Jingsheng begins his eighteenth year in prison. The tumbrels make themselves more visible with the approach of the New Lunar Year.

The folly continues.